THE FUTURE AND THE PAST

Also by Robert Gardner
Kitchen Chemistry
Projects in Space Science
Science Around the House
Science in Your Backyard
(with David Webster)
The Whale Watchers' Guide

THE FUTURE AND THE PAST

Life 100 Years from Now
and 100 Years Ago

ROBERT GARDNER
and
DENNIS SHORTELLE

JULIAN MESSNER

Copyright © 1989 by Robert Gardner and Dennis Shortelle
All rights reserved including the right of
reproduction in whole or in part in any form.
Published by Julian Messner, a division of
Silver Burdett Press, Inc., Simon & Schuster, Inc.,
Prentice Hall Bldg., Englewood Cliffs, NJ 07632.
JULIAN MESSNER and colophon are trademarks of
Simon & Schuster, Inc. Design by Meredith Dunham.
Manufactured in the United States of America.

10 9 8 7 6 5 4 3 2 1

Library of Congress Cataloging-in-Publication Data

Gardner, Robert, 1929–
   The future and the past / Robert Gardner and Dennis Shortelle.
   p.   cm.
   Includes index.
   Summary: Examines social changes in the areas of family life, education, housing, work, fashion, communication, and health over the past 100 years and offers predictions for the future.
   1. Social prediction—Juvenile literature. [1. United States—Social conditions. 2. Forecasting.] I. Shortelle, Dennis. II. Title.
HN17.5.G359   1989
303.4'973—dc19
                                               88–31176
                                                 CIP
                                                  AC

ISBN 0–671–65742–9

CONTENTS

1. Searching the Past and Predicting the Future — 1
2. Family Life and Leisure: Where the Future Is the Past — 11
3. The Changing Nature of Childhood and Education — 30
4. Housing and Architecture: From Farmhouse to Space Colony — 47
5. Work: Whatever Happened to the Iceman? And Would You Like to Drive a Space Tug? — 67
6. Clothing and Fashion: Our Ever-Changing View of What the Well-Dressed Person Should Wear — 84
7. Communication: From the Telegraph to Intergalactic Messages — 98
8. Transportation: From Horse and Buggy to Space Buses — 108

9 Food and Agriculture: From Family Farm to Community Greenhouse 129

10 Health and Medicine: From Patent Medicines to Self-Care and Computerized Diagnoses 146

Books about the Future 162

Books and Articles about the Past 164

Index 166

1

Searching the Past and Predicting the Future

The best prophet of the future is the past.
—*Lord Byron,* Journal

Have you ever wondered what life would have been like if you had been born a hundred years earlier? Your great-great-grandparents might be able to help you, but it's unlikely that they are still alive. However, even though we can't talk to anyone who remembers life as it was that long ago, we can learn how those people lived and even experience the environment in which they lived. We are able to do this by reading the letters our ancestors wrote, as well as the books, newspapers, magazines, and other accounts that were published in the nineteenth century.

From such written records we know how people traveled, what they ate, how they communicated, what they learned, how and where they earned a living, what they did with their leisure time, and how their families were structured. Many of the old homes and factories where these people lived and worked still exist, so we can physically enter the same buildings that they did. At an antiques sale, in an old home, or at a museum we can see the furniture, tools, dishes, toys, clothing, and other objects that they used.

You may wonder, too, what life will be like a century from now. There is no way we can know for certain what the future will hold, but as you will see, we can make educated estimates about possible futures based on the present and the past. That's what makes the future so interesting!

In each chapter of this book we will use history to describe what your life might have been like if you had lived a hundred years ago. Then we will use the methods of futurists to provide an estimate of what life might be like a hundred years from now when the twenty-first century is drawing to a close.

Learning about Our Ancestors

To understand what it was like to live a century ago we make use of the methods developed by social historians. These historians believe that one cannot fully understand the past simply by studying wars, tariffs, the laws passed by Congress, the efforts of former Presidents, or the biographies of national leaders. Such events are important, but so, too, are other details that are not found in most history courses. These include work and leisure, crime and punishment, family roles and functions, attitudes toward life and death, and sexuality. In studying these human concerns, social historians have sought to understand how values and behavior have changed over time.

Social historians are certain that people do not wake up thinking about politics or presidential leadership but rather of their own work, family, vacation, or approaching old age. These researchers do not study the national policymakers or those who were influential in national affairs. They study the faceless masses of people who were affected by the decisions of those elected to high office.

Many common folk of the nineteenth century were illiterate and poorly educated. They did not write or speak for the public record. As a result, the usual sources studied by historians provide little information about them. This lack of data has led social historians to seek alternative sources of information. These include wills, census records, estate inventories, photographs, police records, diaries, gravestones, and other records. Their work has given us a better understanding of these "forgotten" people in our history—members of the working class, women, ethnic groups, children, and the elderly.

To get a sense of how a social historian works, just look at your own room. What could someone learn about you by examining the contents of your room? Or carefully examine and read the label on a soup can. What does such a simple bit of research tell you about life in the modern United States?

Of course, social historians do not ignore the major events that led to social change. For example, industrialism after 1870 had a major impact on American life. So did World War II, which dramatically changed the nation's attitude toward women and their work. To understand the events that initiate trends, changes in attitudes, or alterations in the way we do things, we must examine society by studying large blocks of time. Consequently, while the historical aspect of this book deals primarily with the 1880s and 1890s, much of the information also applies to the 1870s, when the changes began, and on into the early part of the twentieth century prior to World War I.

A Rapidly Changing Present

It is strange but true that we can predict the future of stars, including the sun, for the next billion years far more accurately than we can predict our own future for the next decade. Predicting the future is a very difficult process, and predictions are often inaccurate.

Suppose you were living before the industrial revolution, the shift from an agricultural and handmade products economy to machine and factory production. You could easily predict your future and the future of your children. In those days, modes of behavior, dress, custom, education, transportation, communication, and available jobs remained relatively unchanged from one generation to the next. Farming was the most common occupation in those days. So if you were a boy and your father was a farmer, then it was very likely that you would till the same soil as your father. If you were a girl, you would probably marry a farmer and carry out all the chores expected of a farmer's wife.

Today's ever-changing world is very different. Half the products you see in a supermarket probably weren't there ten years ago. Your parents, grandparents, and great-grandparents have seen remarkable changes in their lifetimes. Your grandparents can probably tell you what life was like before television, air-conditioning, tape recorders, and permanent-press clothing. And your parents can recall life before microwave ovens, digital watches, pocket calculators, personal computers, supersonic transportation, and electronic games. The past century has seen more inventions than in all previous human history.

Predicting the Future

Humans have always been interested in the future, even when their own lives were quite predictable. Kings wanted to know if they could win the wars they planned to wage. Business people wondered if they were making sound investments. Indeed, all people have sought the path to happiness. People often turned to fortune-tellers. Some fortune-tellers would try to predict the future by gazing into a crystal ball. Others looked at the lines in the palm of their questioner's hand or at tea leaves in a cup. Still others tried to predict a person's future by feeling the bumps on his or her head. Usually, the forecasts of fortune-tellers, oracles, and psychics were so ambiguous that they could be interpreted in many ways.

For much of the past 100 years, public interest in the future has been fostered by books and, more recently, by comic strips, movies, magazines, and television shows. Jules Verne's *A Journey to the Center of the Earth* (1864), H. G. Wells's *The War of the Worlds* (1898), the Tom Swift series, magazines such as *Popular Mechanics, Popular Science,* and *Modern Mechanix,* along with comic strip characters such as Buck Rogers and Flash Gordon have provided plenty of reading material about the future for people of all ages. Such movies as *In the Year 2000* (1912), *Things to Come* (1936), *2001: A Space Odyssey* (1968), and *Star Wars* (1977), along with TV shows that include *Captain Video* and *Star Trek*, have provided fictional visions of the future.

Science fiction stories usually take place in the future. Most authors of such books, unlike fortune-tellers, try to be scientifically accurate about the futures they conceive. This has not always been true. In 1888, Edward Bellamy's book, *Looking Backward*, described Boston in the year 2000. Bellamy foresaw an orderly, dignified society where inequalities had been eliminated. The future forecast by Bellamy and the futures predicted by many utopian writers were comforting. These predictions fulfilled the desires of many to return to the cherished values of the past, but they were not accurate. Changes in technology are generally accompanied by social changes and changes in values. Two centuries ago, when the work ethic was paramount, to call someone hardworking was a compliment. Today, because leisure time is so cherished, such a person might be considered a workaholic.

Futurists—people who try to make accurate predictions of the future—use a number of techniques. They begin by gathering information and analyzing it. One method futurists use is the Delphi technique. Futurists ask experts in a particular field such as business or transportation to make predictions about what they think will happen in their field over some specific period of time. The predictions of these experts are then sent to other experts who are asked to review them. After considering the predictions made by others, some experts will revise their own forecasts. Futurists then look to see where the experts agree about the future.

Futurists try to forecast broad social trends as well as changes in a particular field such as business, communication, or transportation.

In addition to the Delphi technique, futurists look for recurring trends or patterns. Then they project the trends into the future, using history and reason to guide them. Usually they provide us with alternative predictions, called *scenarios*. These scenarios are based on many factors, including forecasts of the different ways in which a society may respond to new inventions, discoveries, or trends. For example, if futurists assume that people will decide it's wise and economical to conserve energy, then predictions of how long our fossil fuels will last will be quite different from predictions based on an assumption that people will return to a casual overuse of energy.

Some events may drastically alter the future and change predictions. Certainly no one foresaw the frightening explosion of the space shuttle *Challenger*, an event that changed NASA's timetables for the nation's space program. Things that we think are impossible today may turn out to be not so difficult a century from now. A hundred years ago no one seriously believed that anyone would ever travel faster than sound, walk on the moon, receive a heart transplant, watch the Olympic Games live while seated 12,000 miles from the events, build a weapon that could destroy an entire city, or store the contents of a book on a small floppy disk.

Similarly, brain transplants, telepathic communication, speeds exceeding the velocity of light, and computers that think like humans and reproduce them-

THE FUTURE AND THE PAST 8

selves—all of which we view as impossible today—may be common a century from now.

Predictions of the Future from the Past

In 1900, John E. Watkins predicted some changes that would occur in the twentieth century. Here are his predictions:

Accurate

Machines will be made that will keep food cool and fresh.

People will be larger and will live longer.

Subways will replace streetcars.

Cars will replace horses as a means of transportation.

Gym will become a part of the public school curriculum.

Cameras, screens, and wires will produce pictures that appear to move (movies).

Music will be telephoned (radio).

Spigots (thermostats) will be used in houses to regulate temperature.

Inaccurate

Flies and mosquitoes will be eliminated

The U.S. population will grow to 350–500 million because Mexico and South American countries will join the United States to form one nation.

Strawberries will become as big as apples, and peas will be as large as beets.

Hydropower will replace coal as a source of electricity.

Electric-powered ships moving on skilike runners will cross the ocean in two days.

Food for communities will be cooked in a central place and sent by pneumatic tubes to individual homes.

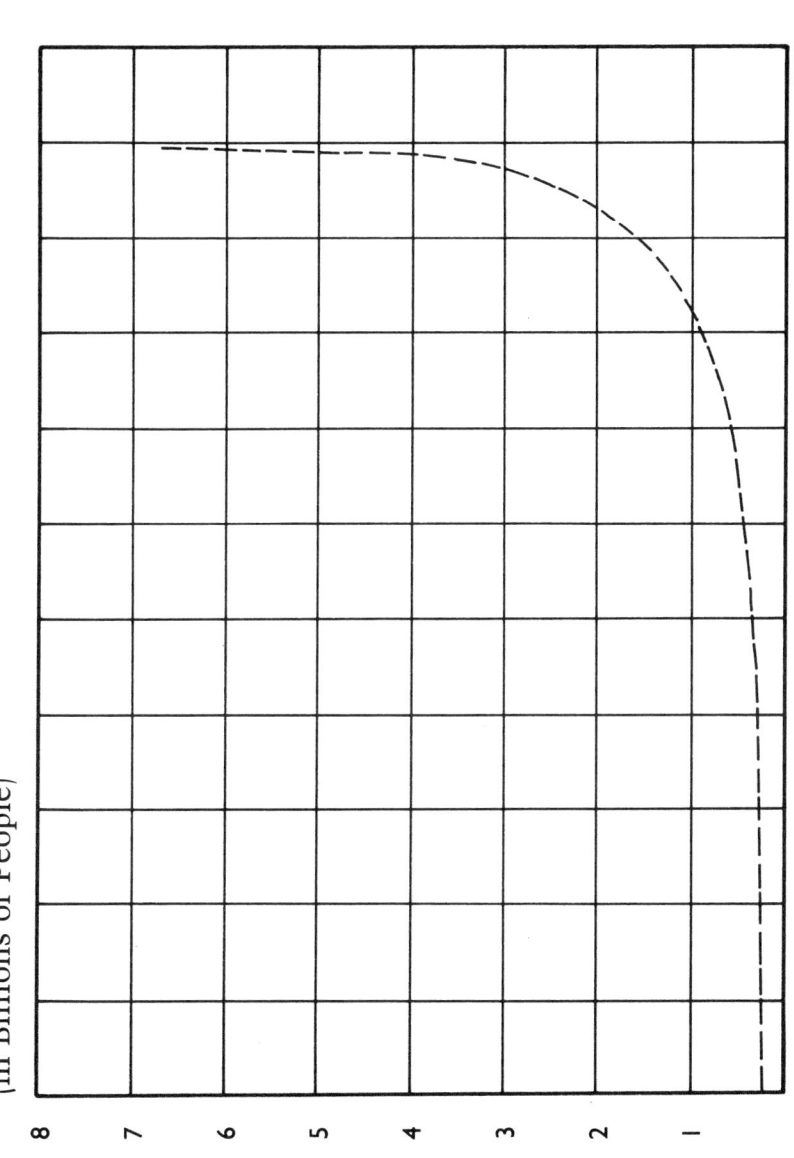

FIG. 1. **World Population Growth.** *Based on this trend in world population, can you predict the population of the world in the year 2000? How about in 2090?*

As you can see, Watkins was sometimes right and sometimes wrong. He could not foresee the ill effects of insecticides and the huge demand for electricity that would require more than could be supplied by dams. Nor could he foresee the unwillingness of nations to give up their independence to join the growing population of the United States or the lack of enthusiasm among people for giant strawberries and peas. (Somehow, in 1900, bigger meant better!)

Even if we assume that futurists can make increasingly accurate predictions of the future, we will still have to make choices. The decisions that we as a society make are based on values, and choosing among values is not easy. For example, we might choose to travel in small, inexpensive, easy-to-operate airplanes or helicopters instead of automobiles. This would make travel faster and reduce the amount of money needed to build and repair highways. However, such transportation would increase both energy demand and the risk of midair collisions.

A severe energy shortage could lead to a law forbidding the use of private automobiles. Such a law would reduce the use of energy, but it would seriously restrict personal freedom. It would also require a vast change in the travel habits of an entire nation as well as a need to develop a larger, more efficient system of public transportation.

On the other hand, the consequences of some decisions are so evident that one need not be a futurist to predict the results. The forecasts for the outcome of a nuclear war, for example, are all so devastating that they are probably the most important factors in preventing such a conflict.

2

Family Life and Leisure: Where the Future Is the Past

We should all be concerned about the future because we will have to spend the rest of our lives there.
—Leo Tolstoy

Early in this nation's history, life focused on the family, which was primarily a working unit. Most work was done at home and the products of that work were of benefit to the family. Life revolved about the family.

During the industrial revolution a new economic arrangement for the nuclear family emerged. The nuclear family is one in which the parents and children live together without grandparents, aunts and uncles, and cousins. While the nuclear family had long existed in the United States, the work roles changed. The father worked outside the home, the mother ran the household, and their children had little idea what their father did in his job. Work shifted from the family farm to the factory as the nation changed from a rural to an urban society.

Today the traditional nuclear family where only the father works outside the home is fast becoming the minority. In many homes both parents work. One-parent families are common, and there are an increasing number of variant family structures.

A century from now an even wider variety of family forms will exist. However, it is likely that the home may once again become the primary workplace in the American economy.

The Family in 1890

By the end of the nineteenth century, the family was no longer the nation's basic economic unit. It had lost that role, and its fabric was strained. The nation rose to industrial prominence, and people migrated from family farms to city factories. The result was that the percentage of people involved in agriculture declined dramatically from about 64 percent in 1850 to about 38 percent in 1900. Home and the workplace became separate as family members left the household to labor in factories or businesses. Peer groups, both adult and child, clubs, and schools competed with the family in providing support, security, and companionship. New leisure activities, ready-made clothes, and the growing individualism of the era further undermined the family as the foundation of the nation's society and economy. Some experts predicted an end to the traditional family. However, though the nature of the family was changing, it remained an influential factor; it did not dissolve.

The typical late nineteenth-century urban American family was *nuclear*—a married couple, with or without children, living by themselves. A small number of people lived in *extended families*, that is, with in-laws or relatives such as grandparents, aunts, uncles, and cousins.

As the birthrate (the number of births per year) declined, families became smaller. Three or four children became the average number per family. With more children living through infancy, parents did not feel it was necessary to have seven or eight children to ensure the survival of the family. Further, in the new industrial society, parents realized that if they had fewer children, they could enjoy a higher standard of living. Fewer children might also enable them, as parents, to be more attentive to the children they did have.

The declining birthrate, however, was of national concern. During the last two decades of the nineteenth century, about 9 million immigrants came to the United States. Many of these immigrants had larger families than did the native middle-class population. Some Americans feared "race suicide," a fear that immigrants would outnumber the white Anglo-Saxon Protestant middle-class majority and change the face of the nation. What Americans did not realize was that immigrants and others in the working class were arriving at the same conclusions as the middle class. The families of working class and immigrant people tended to be larger than average. Nevertheless, their birthrates were declining as well, though at a slower rate. In fact, immigrant families in their desire to become American began to adopt the values of the native middle class.

The decline of the family as an economic unit led to a redefinition of its role in society. The new view of the family and home attempted to recall the sentimental notion of family before industrialization. The family was seen as a shield and refuge from the impersonal world of trade, commerce, and industry. It protected children from that world until they were old enough and well enough equipped, through education and carefully monitored experience, to deal with the hard reality of an economically competitive society. A hardworking father could relax and renew his spirit surrounded by a loving and supportive family. Even the architecture of the home—big, ornate, and fortresslike—lent itself to the notion of the family as a refuge. The rush to the suburbs, a desire to return to peaceful country living away from the workplace, further emphasized the idealistic view of the preindustrial family.

The dominant figure in the family was the father. He was expected to be both leader and breadwinner. It was the father who daily plunged into the industrial-business world. He was the family's main contact with the greater outside world. The home was literally his castle, a place for him to seek asylum from the bewildering forces that assaulted a working man. As the United States became an industrial nation, the father was away from home so much that some of his authority necessarily fell to his wife, who managed the everyday household affairs.

Creating a strong home, a sanctuary against corrupt values and unhealthy influences, and rearing good children were primarily the mother's duty. She was considered uniquely qualified to carry out this mission. Women were regarded as virtuous, with inborn characteristics like gentleness, a higher sense of good, affection, and a special talent for managing children. Women formed the solid foundation of society as the center of the family in a changing, impersonal, and threatening world. This was a woman's great calling. Women who worked outside the home were viewed as having rejected their highest responsibility. Such work was seen as unnecessary and as evidence of domestic failure. Women were supposed to provide for the young a home sheltered from a hard economic world. Yet these same women were generally not exposed to the crass values of industrial society. Although women were vitally important in the home and in rearing children, they were not regarded as the equal of men. By 1896, only four states allowed women to vote. Women were discriminated against by the law. For example, men could sue for divorce based on adultery, but women could not. Men still kept a good deal of control over the person and property of their wives and daughters. These women had no legal right to property, earnings, or children. Though the majority of women accepted their status as the nature of things, some rebelled. In the last years of the nineteenth century, reformers like Victoria Woodhull, Tennessee Claflin, and Susan B. Anthony worked to gain equality for women.

In the home, the woman did the work, and by her home a woman was judged. If her house was unkempt, it was a sure sign that she was not meeting her domestic responsibilities. Shopping was an almost daily chore for women because iceboxes were small and inefficient. Supermarkets were unknown. Shopping was a time-consuming activity involving numerous stops at small markets. Through cooking, a wife daily displayed her ability to care for the family. Meals in 1890 were larger than today's and required more preparation. Housecleaning, washing, sewing, mending, and baking occupied still more of a woman's time. Even improvements in household technology such as the carpet sweeper and vacuum cleaner did not change women's work significantly. The standards of cleanliness and neatness rose accordingly, and the amount of energy required to meet them remained constant.

But a good wife did more than household chores; she was responsible for training and rearing the children. Motherhood was a job for which women were groomed from birth. Medical knowledge reinforced women's role with statistics indicating that women who had children were healthier and happier than childless women, who were subject to a greater chance of feminine diseases. Children were very important to families in the 1880s and 1890s and were regarded as a reflection of the parents, and particularly of the mother's skill in rearing and inspiring them.

In summary, the late nineteenth-century family was in a state of flux. Families in towns and cities became nuclear and smaller than in previous generations. Children were to be loved and fussed over, but they were not to be spoiled. Most important, income was no longer generated in the home, but rather in factories and businesses to which the breadwinner had to travel each day.

Life on the Farm

Family life on the farm in 1890 was closer in structure to the family unit of preindustrial times. Rural families were generally larger than urban families because "many hands make light work."

Family Life and Leisure

School sessions depended on the planting, harvesting, and haying schedules of the farms from which the students came. But children seldom went to school beyond what we now call the elementary level. Girls were needed at home to relieve mothers of their drudgery. Twelve-year-old boys worked beside their fathers in the fields and barns. Even the younger children had chores to do. They would weed the garden, feed the animals, carry wood for the stoves, and drive the cows to and from pasture at milking time.

Evenings in farmhouses were short. The family went to bed early and awakened early to do chores. In those brief evening hours of leisure they might enjoy playing cards, writing letters, and reading the Bible or other books. Another popular pastime was looking through mail-order catalogs and wishing for the items pictured there.

On Saturdays the whole family might climb into the horse-drawn wagon or buggy and head for town. There children would play with town friends. Mother and older daughters would go to stores to shop and to look. Father and older sons would visit local craftsmen if there were items to be repaired. They might also stop at feed, seed, and grain stores to deliver crops or order new materials. Sometimes there would be a visit to a bank to borrow money if the previous year's crop, beef, egg, pork, or milk production had been a lean one.

The annual county fair, which included vocational exhibits and the judging of products from competing farmers, was a means of professional improvement and a treat for the entire family. Farmers entered their best crops and livestock into competition with those of their county neighbors. Farm wives provided their best pies and cakes for the hungry palates of lucky food judges. Children enjoyed the rides, sideshows, and other entertainment.

Two things separated the farmers of the late nineteenth century from their preindustrial ancestors—the mail-order catalog and RFD (Rural Free Delivery) mail. Sears Roebuck and Montgomery Ward mail-order catalogs made it possible for farm families to purchase the conveniences their city relatives owned—if they could afford them. The books were used for everything from reading lessons to wish fulfillment. RFD mail, established in 1896, temporarily relieved the rural isolation by bringing to the farm letters from relatives, the daily newspaper, up-to-date mail-order catalogs, and the products that had been ordered from them.

Newfound Leisure

The separation of home and workplace led to a revolution of sorts. There had always been organized recreation in the United States, but it was usually tied to some form of work celebration such as completing the harvest or the raising of a barn. Labor-saving technology and a shorter workweek allowed workers to set some time aside for leisure activities. To be sure, this was not true for all workers. Farmers and steelworkers, who still labored twelve to fourteen hours between breakfast and supper, were exhausted at day's end. Nevertheless, the majority of Americans in the eighties and nineties faced a dazzling array of options competing for their leisure-time attention. Play became big business in the eighties and nineties.

Family Life and Leisure

One of the major characteristics of the new leisure was that people watched, rather than participated in, their entertainment. The most popular pastime of the era was organized sports, especially baseball. Originally a gentleman's game, by 1869 the aristocratic tone disappeared and baseball was on its way to becoming *the* national pastime. Even if people did not play or watch in person, they could follow the progress of their favorite team through detailed newspaper stories.

Baseball players in 1895. Print: UPI/Bettmann Newsphotos

The 1869 Cincinnati Red Stockings were the first professional team. Players were paid $1,200 to $1,400 for the sixty-six game season! Because the game was later plagued by gambling, fixed games, and arguments about the rules, the National League was formed in 1876 with strict standards for its members. In 1889, after completing the first world tour, the Chicago White Stockings were invited to the White House to meet President Grover Cleveland. By 1890, crowds of sixty thousand people were not unusual at important games.

Baseball was reflective of the industrial age. Its strict rules and emphasis on competition were similar to those of the workplace. The authority figure, the umpire, could be compared to a foreman, but the fans could voice their anger and frustration at the men in blue, something they could not do to foremen in the workplace. Finally, baseball provided a common, unifying experience for many people and allowed them to identify with the home team. This was especially important in large cities, which were so impersonal.

Football was less popular with the masses. It was largely an intercollegiate sport and attracted those who could afford advanced education. Ironically, these refined gentlemen fought one another savagely. Severe injuries were a part of football, and frequent deaths were a blight on the game. It was not until President Theodore Roosevelt stepped in to modify the rules and the Intercollegiate Athletic Association was formed that football gained wider public acceptance.

However, violence as leisure was accepted in the prizefighting ring. The rules of the ring were very casual, and fighting was more like organized brawling. The last bare-knuckle championship fight was in July 1889 when John L. Sullivan, the Boston Strong Boy, successfully defended his heavyweight title in a grueling seventy-five round match against Jake Kilrain. For his efforts, Sullivan received $20,000 and a diamond-studded belt and became the most popular boxer of the day. Boxing was changing by that time as more civilized rules were introduced, creating the sport that Americans are familiar with today.

Tennis and golf, which the press and public referred to as "cowpasture pool," also became popular in the eighties and nineties, though with a smaller group. The first golf course was established in 1888 at St. Andrew's Golf Club in Yonkers, New York. Tennis arrived from Bermuda in 1874. The original idea was to create a sport that could be enjoyed by women in long dresses as well as by men. While both sports had their supporters, neither generated a large following. Both required expensive equipment and large playing areas, which were not available except at private country clubs.

Though most sports were enjoyed mainly by men, the two greatest crazes of the age, bicycling and croquet, appealed to both sexes. These activities provided opportunities for recreational companionship that broke the stiff formality of a Sunday visit. Also, after women began to ride bicycles and play croquet, tennis, and golf, they began to demand dress reform. The greasy sprocket on a bicycle, torn hems from the rough of a golf course, and a desire for freedom of motion in tennis contributed to changes in women's styles.

THE FUTURE AND THE PAST 22

Women's colleges emphasized physical as well as academic development. Women students participated in rowing, swimming, and track. Eventually basketball, invented as a winter sport for men in 1891, became the most popular physical activity for women.

Show business also profited from Americans' search for amusement. Almost every town had a theater or opera house, and promoters filled them regularly with traveling shows. Serious theater companies presented plays by

Bicycle riding reached a peak of popularity in the 1890s.
Print: UPI/Bettmann Newsphotos

Family Life and Leisure

Shakespeare, and no one interpreted the Bard better than Edwin Booth. Booth, the brother of John Wilkes Booth, Lincoln's assassin, became the leading actor of the period. However, Shakespeare was too refined for most people's taste. Melodramas and vaudeville were more popular.

The melodrama of the time had a simple plot and stereotyped characters who were easily identified. Villains were dressed in black and had black mustaches. Heroes were strong, good-looking, and hardworking. Of course, there was always a naive heroine who needed to be saved, and good eventually triumphed over evil.

Vaudeville was a cleaned-up version of burlesque, the suggestive variety shows popular in bars and saloons. Magicians, singers, dancers, ventriloquists, and other performers filled out a nine-act show. Kar Mi, a contortionist on the vaudeville circuit, would swallow the butt of a gun, fire it, and hit a target held by an assistant.

Circuses were ever popular. Prior to the Civil War, they were regional businesses, but improvements in the railroads allowed the larger ones to travel nationally. P. T. Barnum, whose statement, "There's a sucker born every minute!" became a slogan for many entrepreneurs, had the best-known circus. By 1888, Barnum had lost control of the business, and eventually the circus was taken over by the Ringling brothers.

Although people enjoyed public forms of entertainment, a good deal of leisure activity remained home-centered. Music lessons, especially piano lessons, were popular. Family reading increased, and publishers produced more books. Fiction and religious books were especially popular. A historical novel like *Ben-Hur* (1880), which combined both, was a guaranteed best-seller.

In the last two decades of the nineteenth century, people spent more time in a wide variety of leisure pursuits. Leisure had become a major part of American life.

The Family in 2090

In some ways family life in the late twenty-first century may be more similar to that of the early nineteenth century than to that of the late nineteenth or the twentieth century. By 2090 a large segment of the population will be working at home. Even today we hear of the "electronic cottage"—a home that is connected to a central office through a computer. Many secretaries, writers, accountants, bookkeepers, journalists, and others work this way today. As jobs become more information-oriented and as communication becomes far less expensive than transportation, it makes good sense, in terms of both efficiency and economy, to have people work at home. Employees working at home can choose their own working hours and can avoid the cost of commuting to a job where they would probably sit at a computer terminal anyway.

By allowing employees to work at home, companies can cut their operating expenses by reducing office and parking space, furniture, equipment, taxes, and cleaning costs.

Though face-to-face meetings are often essential in business, industry, education, and government, in 2090 such contacts will most often be accomplished by way of TV-telephones and computers that will allow teleconferencing through multiline hookups.

As a result of this growing trend for people to work at home, the demand for day-care centers will decline. More children will grow up with their parents or guardians close by most of the time. Though the nature of the work will be quite different from what it was in the rural homes of the early nineteenth century, the fact that it can be done at home will create a similar family environment. Children and parents will be in closer contact for longer periods of time. Children will feel less peer pressure, will be expected to do more of the household chores, and will be far more aware of their parents' work than are children today. The family will again become an economic unit.

Despite the similarity of the homes of the future to the homes of the past, there will be differences, too. Families will be more diverse. The traditional nuclear family—father, mother, and children—will be less common than it is now. The kinds of family groups in evidence today—which include a single parent, grandparents, unmarried parents, and so forth—will increase in number. However, there will be a return to more extended families a century from now. More couples will decide not to have children, and several couples may share housing to reduce costs. Two or more families, related or unrelated, may live in the same house because they work together. Married children may live with one or both parents to reduce living costs. Further, as is often true of the future, there may be family units that we cannot even anticipate today.

As robots take over the repetitious work in factories and homes, the work performed by people will require more education, creativity, and thought. As a result, most people will find their work more abstract, interesting,

and take realistic trips to any part of the world. A laser disk trip displayed on a large, clear TV screen will be so realistic that you will feel as though you are flying over, or walking or riding through, the region. To add to the realism, you will hear the sounds, smell the odors, and feel the temperature and humidity of the area you are "visiting." You will also be able to talk to people playing the roles of important historical figures—Washington, Jefferson, Lincoln, Roosevelt, Hitler, and others. Imagine the excitement in being able to talk with Abraham Lincoln about his views on slavery or asking Franklin Roosevelt how he dealt with the Great Depression of the 1930s.

Sports will remain an important part of most youngsters' lives. Each child will be tested quite early for peripheral vision, oxygen intake, muscle strength, predominance of muscle fiber type, and so forth. After the results have been analyzed through a computer program, children will be encouraged to pursue those sports best suited to their body type, innate abilities, and interest.

Because most work will require the use of the mind rather than the body, people will devote more time to exercise and work about the home that will keep them physically fit. An emphasis on a balance of body and mind, head and hand, abstract and concrete, objective and subjective will be clearly evident in this home-oriented future society. Since the computer will allow many people to work at home, home can be wherever the family chooses. Quality of life and environment will be more important than income to most people.

Family Economics

The family computer will maintain contact with the bank so that a push of a key will provide an up-to-date account of the family's financial status. By means of computer contact with a bank, cable television displays of merchandise, and TV telephones that allow people to view materials while they talk with a sales clerk, families of the future will be able to do all their shopping at home. There may be some delay during the holiday season, but shopping from a comfortable couch will certainly beat fighting the crowds.

A century ago schools had replaced the family as the source of a child's education. These schools were designed to prepare youngsters for the routine of the factory. Students sat in rows where they were taught to be punctual, to follow a fixed schedule, to be obedient, and to learn by rote. By 2090 many families will work at home, and children will have a role in the family economy. Some of their education will take place in the home, and rewards will go to those who think clearly and creatively rather than to those who follow directions learned by rote. In effect, the family of tomorrow will require those qualities found in the farm families that preceded the industrial revolution. They will provide for their elders, educate their children who will work part-time for the family, and grow a substantial portion of their own food in family or community gardens.

3

The Changing Nature of Childhood and Education

*Whosoever neglects learning in his youth
Loses the past and is dead for the future
—Euripides,* Phrixus *fragment*

In preindustrial America children were part of the family economic unit. The boys worked beside their father in the fields and the girls beside their mother in the house and garden. Most of their education, what little there was, was obtained by the family hearth.

The idea of childhood as a separate phase of life became established in the nineteenth century. It was during this same time that the idea of universal education became popular.

By 2090 children may once again play an active role in the family's work. Unlike most children today, tomorrow's youth will be aware of what their parents do to earn a living, because they will have a share in it as they join the family work force in the home. Once again a large part of their education will take place at home. However, it will be the computer's capacity to individualize education, not a disdain for "book learning," that will return schooling to the home.

Childhood in Early Nineteenth-Century United States

Childhood in the early 1800s was difficult. Because of intestinal diseases, infections, and contagious diseases such as measles and mumps, deaths among infants were common. About 30 percent of newborns died before they reached the age of five, and about half of all children died before they reached their late teens. Some parents were reluctant to become emotionally attached to an infant before it had a reasonable chance of survival. The care of infants posed a real hardship for a farm family because often women were needed to work beside their husbands in the fields. Pregnancy and childbirth limited a woman's contribution to the family's well-being. Children were considered selfish and self-centered because of the attention and time they demanded. They had to be made to realize as soon as possible that the family unit was more important than any one individual. Discipline was harsh. The traditional feeling was that young children took from the family and contributed nothing until they could work.

If infants survived to the age of seven, they were expected to work on the farm or in the home and learn from their parents. Boys sometimes became apprentices to craftsmen. Children took on adult work quickly and were expected to aid the family financially.

There were no specific clothes for children. They dressed like miniature adults and were treated as such.

The few toys found in a family home were handmade. Schooling was not required and was sporadic at best. Children, it was felt, learned best at home. The family was the source of education, companionship, and work.

Changes in Attitude Toward Childhood

The 1880s and 1890s were a period of child-centeredness and permissiveness. By this time families were moving away from farms to take jobs in factories and businesses in cities and towns. Many physical tasks of rural life were no longer necessary. Industrialism required skills considered too difficult or too dangerous for most middle-class children. The economic role of children in the family declined, at least until a boy or girl reached the teenage years, and childhood, for most children, lasted longer. Compulsory education, first adopted by Massachusetts in 1852, was gradually accepted. Play and school, not work, became the main concerns of upper- and middle-class children in the last two decades of the nineteenth century. Industries that catered to a more carefree youth began to develop and prosper. Books, toys, furniture, and clothes designed especially for children were widely available, thanks to new manufacturing techniques and better transportation. Although the family remained central in a child's life, there were assaults on its authority from schools, peer groups, and experts such as educators, psychologists, and others who sought to help parents rear their children.

Most, but not all, children enjoyed a better life in the eighties and nineties. Child labor remained the shame of

The Changing Nature of Childhood and Education

a country where a poor child could earn only very low wages in factories where the demand for unskilled labor was unceasing. But the new attitude toward children led men like Jacob Riis and Lewis Hine, who were photographers and journalists, to bring the ugliness of a child's life in factories and slums to the attention of the American people and to spark the call for child labor reform.

Although it was the middle class that first embraced the concern for children of the poor, the working class followed their lead. To be sure, the new attitude toward childhood was applied more readily to girls than to boys. Nevertheless, parental concern for all children became widely accepted during this period.

A key to the improved childhood of your great-grandparents was the realization that children had special needs and were not miniature adults. Simplicity and innocence were considered characteristic of children. It was felt that childhood should be a cheerful time, since happiness was believed to be essential for future emotional balance and economic success. Childhood came to be regarded as a separate and very special time of life. The nursery, a child's special place, became a part of many middle-class homes. Kindergartens, established in the United States in 1889, provided organized play for children and also prepared them for school and eased them gradually into education.

The responsibility for developing sound character in children was placed squarely on the parents. This it was believed could best be accomplished through reason, love, and emotional support. Physical punishment came to be considered old-fashioned and used only as a last resort.

Guidance was the proper role of mothers and fathers in dealing with their children. Parents were encouraged to respond to their children's needs without concern for spoiling them.

Better Health Care for Children

This increasing affection and concern for children resulted in advances in children's health care. By the end of the nineteenth century, the infant death rate had been reduced to about 5 percent. In 1880 pediatrics (medical care for children) was established as a special branch of medicine. Hospitals and clinics that provided advice to mothers before and after they gave birth became common in most urban areas. Better training for midwives, nurses, and doctors also contributed to improved rates of survival among children. Infant nutrition improved with the introduction of special baby foods and city inspections designed to detect impure milk.

Though no one gave any thought to air pollution, long-established garbage dumps, breeders of infection, were being displaced by incinerators after 1885. Though air quality continued to decline as these incinerators burned, there was, at last, a growing awareness that sanitation had to be improved.

After the infant-survival rate began to improve, the birthrate among the middle class declined. With fewer children to manage, parents spent more time taking care of their offspring. In fact, society came to expect parents, especially mothers, to pay greater attention to the health of their children. Childhood deaths were no longer accepted as fate. When a death occurred, it might reflect poor parenting skills. As a result, advice manuals for parents became best-sellers.

Education and Play

Responsible parents were expected to channel their children's play into constructive learning that prepared them for adulthood. Toys for children were linked to the roles they would assume when they grew up. Infant and toddler dolls replaced adult dolls. In this way girls could play "mother" and thus learn what society expected them to know. Girls also learned about homemaking through play. Their introduction to cooking often came as an extension of play rather than as an important contribution to family welfare. Since boys' vocational options were much more diverse, their toys were more varied.

For both girls and boys, the stereoscope, an early instrument for looking at photographs, was another example of instructive entertainment. For each picture, the two plates used with the viewer had been taken from points of view a little bit apart. The stereoscope combined the two into one image to give a three-dimensional effect. The stereographs, or pictures, were usually views of nature, foreign lands, works of art, or other educational subjects. Card games such as author cards, in which players matched authors with the titles of their books, mixed learning with fun and required a good memory rather than mere chance to win.

Children's books and magazines often included games and puzzles, but there was always some lesson to be learned. Fiction and history articles were found in such children's magazines as *St. Nicholas*. The best-known teacher of values was Horatio Alger, whose novels provided not only a story but indirect instruction as well. Alger used one plot with only the names and details changed to achieve his objective. A sample of his titles—*Struggle Upward, Brave and Bold, Luck and Pluck*—reflects his messages. The industrious, pious, thrifty, and brave hero always triumphed over the lazy and selfish villain. The Horatio Alger Awards are given annually to ten Americans who have risen to prominence from a lowly start. Interestingly, Alger's heroes were always boys. Evidently his formula for success did not apply to girls!

By the last decades of the nineteenth century, school became a common experience for children as a stepping stone to adulthood. By virtue of their location outside the home, schools helped to separate adults from children. Schools enhanced the notion that children should be protected and supervised before entering the adult world. Schools also served to assimilate immigrants into American society. A well-rounded education that included a knowledge of the country's history was considered essential for an informed electorate. Textbooks supplied a patriotic, nostalgic, out-of-date image of the United States as a country of farmers and artisans with no mention of industrialism or immigration.

Schools not only provided a common educational base for all citizens. They also sought to reinforce and, if need be, realign values taught at home. Demands of the household and work did not always allow parents to be as at-

The Changing Nature of Childhood and Education

tentive as they should to the moral and intellectual development of their children. Schools, therefore, often performed those tasks. The popular McGuffey readers were used in many schools of the day. They emphasized the importance of education, hard work, patriotism, and consideration for others. Educators believed that this was especially important for schools to teach at a time when industrialism was reshaping society and large numbers of immigrants were arriving daily.

Not everyone was pleased with American schools as the nineteenth century drew to a close. Roman Catholics felt the values taught in public schools were those of a

One-room schoolhouse in a Montana mining town. Photo: Library of Congress

Protestant majority, and in 1884, they began to establish their own parochial (parish) schools.

Schools served as a bridge between the sheltered confines of the family and the harsh reality of the adult working world. They allowed pupils to meet other children from many different backgrounds, and they prepared the young for their roles in an industrial United States.

Advances in technology required workers to learn how to read instructions, directions, and notices. To teach vocational skills, shop courses were established for boys and home economics classes for girls. In school, children also learned self-discipline, punctuality, and attentiveness. These work habits could later be useful on the job, and they were the kind of work habits that a growing industrial nation demanded.

For working families, compulsory education and regulation of child labor presented difficulties. Working mothers had to either quit their jobs or leave their children unattended after school. Required attendance at schools led to financial stress among many poor families who needed the income of their children to survive. As a result, many working parents urged their children, especially the boys, to leave school as soon as possible.

The Emergence of the Teenager

During the 1890s, the American teenager emerged. Traditionally, there were two stages of life, childhood and adulthood. However, increased schooling and the new attitude toward children led to a longer childhood, which forced a redefinition of life's stages. Young people were remaining at home and depending on their parents for finan-

The Changing Nature of Childhood and Education 39

cial support for longer periods of time, especially those whose educational expectations and needs extended beyond elementary school. Children of the late nineteenth century were supposed to be sheltered, nurtured, and guided. Yet this seemed inappropriate for older children who were physically and intellectually mature. This changing relationship between parents and their older children was new to the United States, and people sought to understand it.

The word "adolescence" came into popular use in the United States partly through the work of G. Stanley Hall. He is regarded as the founder of child psychology. He wrote important books on childhood (1883) and adolescence (1904). His studies of adolescence, the mid to late teen years, recognized the difficulties faced by physically mature children who were not yet considered fully adult. (The word "teenager" was still in the distant future and first used in the late 1930s.) Hall helped explain why the parent-child relationship, marked by tolerance and affection for young children, became more difficult as the children became physical and mental adults. Hall defined adolescence as a period of "storm and stress" marked by a lack of emotional control, violent impulses, unreasonable conduct, and lack of enthusiasm. Experts offered several explanations for adolescent storm and stress. In the struggle to find their own identity, youth rejected parental protection and concern as unnecessary.

Most parents in 1890 had never had the choices that their children had with regard to career and life-style. There were all kinds of alternatives for the young people of the day, and making choices was difficult. Finally, adolescents realized their world was separate from that of adults and children. They socialized more with others their age than had previous generations, establishing an identity with them. Do you think the view of adolescence has changed over the past hundred years?

Juvenile Delinquency

Crime in the last twenty-five years of the nineteenth century and crime today share some interesting similarities. As early as 1870 it was considered unsafe to walk in many parts of New York City at night. Central Park was regarded as a particularly dangerous area.

There were three major developments related to crime during that era. The first was the designation of juvenile delinquency as a separate crime category. The second was the rise of professional police forces. Third, a change in the definition of crime led to a public view of the United States as a nation overwhelmed by lawlessness.

The designation of juvenile delinquency as a new crime category led to a greater awareness of crimes committed by youths. Crimes of the young had always been a concern of society. However, during the last two decades of the nineteenth century crimes committed by young people seemed to increase at an alarming rate. Gangs, similar to those in major cities today, with names like the Dead Rabbits, the Bowery Boys, the Smashers, and the Rats harassed citizens, fought turf wars, and robbed at will. Juveniles posed a major problem for the police.

Responsible citizens loudly expressed their concern. Fearing the corruption of the next generation, they de-

The Changing Nature of Childhood and Education

manded action. At first, in keeping with the "modern" attitude toward children, reformers blamed the city environment, lower-class immigrants, or heredity for the increase of young criminals. Children themselves were not held responsible, and so special courts and reform schools were established to deal with the problem.

Eventually, as youth crime statistics grew, juvenile delinquency was tied to the idea of adolescence as a stage in life. After all, people said, adolescence was a time of emotional turmoil and moral confusion that was beyond the control of the adolescents themselves. How would you explain the high crime rate among teenagers today?

It was generally agreed that strict adult supervision was the best solution to the problem. Youth groups, the YMCA, police-sponsored activities, and, later, the Boy Scouts of America provided structured and disciplined ways for youths to release their energy. New laws banning the sale of cigarettes and alcohol to children were passed by state legislatures. Police were given more authority in dealing with adolescents. Loitering and malicious mischief were treated as criminal offenses. Such activities as rock throwing and the vandalism of vacant buildings, which had been tolerated in the past, became unlawful.

Attitudes toward children tend to go in cycles. In 1900 there was a return to strict standards and the belief that children could be molded by parents. But in the late 1940s, Dr. Benjamin Spock's views on permissive child rearing were the rule. Then, in the 1950s, the strict attitude returned. How would you characterize the attitude toward children and child rearing today? Will your generation be the one to change the cycle once again?

THE FUTURE AND THE PAST

Children in 2090

We tend to associate education with childhood, but a century from now education will be a lifelong process. Even today, many professional people return to school periodically so as to keep up with changes in their field. Surgeons observe new operations and techniques. Engineers examine new methods of construction, new chemical processes, and new electrical circuits. Secretaries are trained to use word processors and electronic filing procedures. Automobile mechanics attend classes to learn about the new-model cars that are introduced each year.

A century from now the rate of change will be so rapid in all kinds of technology that continual learning and retraining will be a part of everyone's career. Though infancy probably will change little over the next century, there will be dramatic changes in the way young children are educated. In an effort to provide equal opportunity for all children, regardless of economic status, children will enter school earlier, probably at age three. That will mean that all very young children will have a similar early educational experience.

As the cost of computers falls and as teachers' salaries and taxes continue to rise, computer companies will spend more money on educational research that will lead to increased sales and profits. That is because more computers and fewer teachers will instruct students. Advances in computer technology, artificial intelligence, and brain physiology will provide us with a better understanding of how children learn, think, and imagine. With a better grasp of the learning process, computer companies will develop educational programs to help children learn more effectively and efficiently than they do today. The reason is that the instruction will be individualized to meet the particular learning style of the child. One company is already using a computer with a "voice" to teach primary school children how to read.

Teachers will become "learning coordinators." They will develop an individual program for each student, since research shows that people learn in different ways. The teacher's job will be to guide children into the learning programs that will best fit their learning style and needs. Computers, which are infinitely patient, will be able to tutor students in the manner best suited to their individual learning styles. Because children will be taught basic skills on an individualized basis using methods best suited to their learning mode and interests, they will find learning easier and more fun.

Post-Primary School Childhood

By the time they have finished the primary grades, at about age eight, children will be able to read, write, speak, and listen effectively. With these basic skills they will have the tools needed to learn arithmetic, typing, geography, history, foreign languages, and more sophisticated reading and writing in their own homes with the help of personal computers. These home computers will be linked through fiber optic lines to a mainframe computer at the local education center.

The students' programs will be prepared at the education center by teams of teachers, writers, computer programmers, artists, actors, and producers.

Students will attend school with other children perhaps twice a week. At school they will exchange ideas with teachers and with other students, and conduct laboratory activities. They will also discuss subject matter that requires qualitative evaluation such as literature, social studies, and other subjects in the humanities. While at school, they will meet with their teacher-adviser. He or she will provide the students with learning tools, including computer programs, data bases, laser disks, films, trips to museums and libraries, meetings with special resource teachers or volunteer professionals, and get-togethers with other students who have particular talents.

Through a combination of laser disk, computer, holographic, telephone, and television technology students will have access to a great variety of educational programs. If you were to study history in 2090, you would be able to conduct a "live" interview with Abraham Lincoln and ask him about his views on slavery or discuss with Harry Truman his reasons for deciding to use the atomic bomb to end World War II. As a foreign language student, you would have "phone pals" as well as pen pals. You would be able to see and talk with students in France, Spain, Germany, the Soviet Union, China, and other parts of the world through TV-telephone signals relayed by satellites.

From ages ten through fourteen emphasis will be placed on information and skills needed to use the rapidly changing technology of the late twenty-first century. Education will not be divided up into subject matter such as history, mathematics, science, and so forth. Instead, the use of numerical data and logic in thinking, inquiring, analyzing, and problem solving will be stressed.

Some teenagers may elect to attend special schools. There students may pursue an interest in science, computers, art, literature, foreign language, or perhaps other subjects that are unknown today. Working with students and teachers who share a similar enthusiasm, they will expand their writing, thinking, and problem-solving skills in the specialty of their choosing.

A year or two into their special program these students will begin to apply their learning in a part-time job with one of the companies that sponsor the specialized education. As they grow older, they will spend more time working and less time in school. However, there will never be an abrupt separation between work and education. For as long as they work, these people will continue to study and learn in the never-ending task of staying abreast of changes in their vocation or profession.

Living in Tomorrow's Society

Children will live in stable, closely knit neighborhoods, and they will develop close friendships. The computer's capacity to replace transportation with communication, a change that will allow people to work at home, will increase the number of people living in places that they, not their employer, choose. The closeness and greater permanence of communities in 2090 will provide a setting more like 1890 than 1990. The aim of the 4-H Club—to improve the head, heart, hands, and health—will apply to children a century from now. Their education (head) will be a vital and important part of their lives, but so will their work (hands). Work will be a part not only of their education but of their home and community as well. They will help their parents with household responsibilities, and they will serve their communities by assisting the elderly, working with younger children, and keeping the environment clean and healthful. Sports, both team and individual, will keep them healthy and build their character (heart).

Extended families that include grandparents, together with closer knit communities, will mean that young and old will see more of one another than they do today. The elderly will help children in schools, community work, and play. The young will help the aged with visits and friendship that will include reading to them, playing cards and other games with them, and accompanying them on short trips within the community.

Growing up in a close and caring neighborhood of friends, coupled with an awareness of the plight of people in other lands made possible by electronic media, will probably lead many young people to spend a year or more of their lives in a Peace Corps-like program. These programs will enable them to use their skills to help the people in poor countries attain a better standard of living.

In a world grown small by advances in communication and transportation, the reduced threat of war will allow young people to use their energy to help, not fight, those in other countries.

4

Housing and Architecture: From Farmhouse to Space Colony

The future enters into us, in order to transform itself in us, long before it happens.
—Rainer Maria Rilke, Letter to a Young Poet

That one's home is one's castle was never more true than in the late 1880s when housing conditions improved. The ideal, a home of one's own, was both easier and less expensive to build as a result of technological progress. However, the homes of a century ago will seem primitive indeed to those who will live in the computer-controlled homes that will be common a century from now.

The House of 1890

The most important development was the use of the balloon frame—still the most common method of home construction in the United States today. First used in the 1830s, the balloon frame consists of two-by-four studs with horizontal and diagonal supports, held together with plenty of nails. By the 1870s, balloon framing had become the standard method of home construction in the United States. Its use led builders to more rapidly construct the large, ornate homes that became common in the 1880s.

Architecturally this was the age of spindles, porches, and decorative woodwork. Though styles tended to overlap, three types seemed most fashionable and can still be seen today. First was the Shingle, easily identified by the unpainted wooden shingles that covered the entire home. Homes built in the Shingle Style had the weathered look so celebrated along the New England coast. The roof swept down over a cavelike porch and was supported by stone columns or shingled-wood posts.

The Colonial Revival home, inspired by the 1876 Centennial celebration, was characterized by oversize dormers, porches, and a wide entryway. Colonial Revival houses were much larger and more ornate than the homes of the Colonial period. Columns and large three-part windows on either side of the doorway were also typical of the style.

The Queen Anne home was distinctive in its use of a number of materials—shingles of various shapes, clapboard, and brick—all in one structure. Its very irregular shape, combined with turrets, towers, and wraparound porches, made the style the most varied and decoratively rich of the age. The Queen Anne is the house most clearly identified with the late 1800s.

Approaching such a middle-class house, most modern

A Queen Anne type home popular from about 1875–1910.

Americans would be particularly impressed by the front door. By the 1870s, the upper panel of this door was often made of stained glass. Today, stained glass is usually associated with wealth and luxury, but at that time it was a basic element of home construction. Smaller stained-glass windows in the dining room, bathroom, and along the staircase, offered privacy with light while providing a decorative blind to the hustle and bustle of the outside world.

Though the exteriors of homes were frequently very different, interior floor plans were often quite similar. Guests were greeted in the wide front hall, the most public area of the house. This was an important part of the home, not just a passageway. There were usually a couple of chairs against the wall where people could sit while removing boots or waiting for callers. The hall stand was a dominant piece of furniture. It contained a mirror that allowed guests to check their appearance before being presented to the family. The hall stand served also as a coat rack, and as a table where visitors could leave their calling cards when the family was away.

The Parlor: Where the Elite Met
Off the front hall was the parlor, the showplace of the home. No room was more cared for or fussed over. It was furnished so as to display a family's wealth, dignity, and civility. It was the woman's equivalent of her husband's office, a place to receive visitors and a place where it was permissible to show off a bit. The parlor was designed not for comfort but for fulfilling numerous, required functions. It was here that the family was on display at tea parties, receptions, and, sadly, family funerals.

Formal behavior was expected in the parlor. Children were instructed to be seen but not heard! For some men, time spent in the parlor was boring, a labor they endured for their wives' sake. Etiquette manuals of the day focused on parlor conduct. Such guides went so far as to describe how to properly enter and leave the room. Even conversation was subject to rigid rules. For example, it was considered rude for men to talk of politics since it was assumed women were uninformed or uninterested. (Remember, prior to the passage of the Nineteenth Amendment to the Constitution, in 1920, women in most states

Housing and Architecture

were not permitted to vote.) Friendly arguments were frowned upon, and talking about oneself or one's problems was taboo. Weather was an acceptable topic, however, as were fashions, illnesses, and domestic problems.

"Mind-boggling" might best describe the decor of the nineteenth-century parlor. The room was as ornate as the exterior of the home. Popular publications like *Ladies' Home Journal* (first published in 1883) and *Home Decoration* (1886) kept the housewife informed of the newest trends in interior design. Wallpaper, first used in the 1840s, was utilized lavishly in the 1880s. Parlors traditionally combined a number of different wallpapers. Nature and Oriental designs were the most popular. Even the ceilings were papered in some homes.

Nearly all available floor space was filled. Chairs were designed specifically for men or for women. Large throne-like armchairs allowed men to lean back and relax. Chairs were designed without arms to accommodate women's full skirts and to remind the gentler sex that they were expected to sit with their hands neatly folded in their laps. Rockers were also popular in the 1880s. Other furniture was large, thickly upholstered, and usually covered with horsehair or patterned fabric that complemented the wallpapers. Antimacassars were placed on the chair arms to protect them from wear, and on the back to prevent staining from the grease men used in their hair. Another major piece in many homes was the piano. This instrument demonstrated cultural refinement and also served to draw the family together in frequent sing-alongs. In the summer the furniture was usually draped with cotton slipcovers to protect it from the sun.

There was no single style of furniture. The average home contained a mix-and-match arrangement of currently popular styles and fashionable pieces from previous generations.

With the essentials established by custom, the homemaker was free to personalize the room in small ways. Potted plants were often set in tall vases or hip-high wicker containers. This greenery added a restful element to the parlor. Here one could find also many of the family's prized possessions—souvenirs of trips, photographs, knicknacks, pewter, silver, china plates, and cups—all artistically grouped and arranged by the homemaker. The mantel and piano were usually the places chosen for these displays, which made the feather duster an essential domestic tool.

Parlor decorations also revealed a family's interest in fine art. The works of John Rogers, engineer turned sculptor, were among the most popular pieces of the era. Rogers made his reputation with Civil War sculptures but successfully shifted to works based on everyday American life after the war. These items, priced at five to fifty dollars, depending on size, could be purchased through mail order. Often, portraits of ancestors lent a personal stamp to the room. They were hung beside popular Currier & Ives prints of family scenes and rural landscapes. Larger parlors sometimes included a favorite work of art displayed on an easel.

There was no wall-to-wall carpeting in the 1880s, but Oriental rugs, supplemented by area rugs, were common. Most floors were made of pine or oak boards. Parquet—squares of contrasting hardwoods—also became popular

Housing and Architecture

at this time. Many homes contained fireplaces, but they were primarily decorative. By the mid 1880s, central steam heat had become popular in cities and suburbs. Radiators, painted to complement a room's decor, were found throughout the house. Nevertheless, houses were generally cool. To stay warm in the winter most people wore a "union suit"—a type of underwear with long sleeves and long legs.

A Place to Dine

The dining room became popular in the nineteenth century. Prior to this time, meals were served wherever space

Lunch at the nineteenth-century table. Photo: Culver Pictures, Inc.

allowed, most often in the kitchen. By the 1880s, the dining room was the second most important room in the house—an extension of the parlor. Through manners, decoration, fine china, and silver, a family further displayed its wealth and station in society. In the center of the room stood a large expandable table of oak or mahogany. Decorating magazines advised homeowners to use chairs with either rush or leather seats, which were easy to clean and did not absorb food odors. Wallpaper was not used in the dining room where, for practical reasons, the walls were painted or wood-paneled. Ornately carved sideboards and large china closets were used to store flatware, linens, serving dishes, china, and crystal.

A Not So Modern Kitchen
Next to the dining room was the kitchen. A large window with a view of the backyard allowed natural light to enter. A back porch attached to the kitchen provided a cool place to do kitchen chores in the heat of summer. Because the kitchen was a place to work, it was not decorated and was unremarkable by today's standards. Enamel paint, usually cream-colored or light green, was used to make cleaning easier. There were closets and built-in cupboards with windowed doors to encourage cleanliness and neatness. Dominating the room, four to five feet tall, was the iron monster—the stove. Most stoves burned coal or wood, but in some homes the monster had been modified to burn gas. Many stoves, however, were capable of using other fuel in case of a gas failure. This kitchen beast's demand for heavy-to-carry coal or wood contributed to aching backs and produced stifling heat.

Housing and Architecture

A large icebox, two to three feet across and five feet high, required frequent visits from an iceman. (Blocks of ice were cut from lakes in the winter. The ice was packed in sawdust for insulation and stored in tall buildings called ice houses.) The kitchen also contained a steel or zinc sink with a hand pump that lifted water from a well. The sink could be removed and emptied off the back porch. Water had to be heated in a kettle on the stove. By the turn of the century, this type of sink was slowly being replaced by the version we use today with hot and cold water spigots.

Upstairs to the Bedrooms

Compared with the downstairs, the upper floor of the home was very plain and simple. A good housewife was advised to keep furniture and decorations to a minimum or risk the danger of infection from germs lurking in upholstery or in carved wooden pieces. The major room upstairs was the master bedroom. The best furniture was there, though it was seldom the most fashionable, and was most likely inherited from previous generations, especially since so little expense was spared on the parlor.

Bedroom furniture of a century ago was different from today's in a number of ways. First, built-in closets did not become common until the turn of the century. As a result, the master bedroom often contained a bureau, a dresser, and a large mirror-fronted wardrobe. There was also a washstand with a pitcher and basin—a standard bedroom fixture until the turn of the century. Even after it had ceased to be a necessity, the washstand often remained as a decorative piece. With only one bathroom, family members were expected to wash in their own rooms. Finally, because of the high ceilings and cold floors, the bed was often quite tall, so that the mattress was three to four feet above the floor. For cleanliness, brass or iron beds were preferred to decoratively carved wooden beds. Since the master bedroom sometimes had to double as a sitting room when various functions took over the lower floor, it usually contained a number of wooden chairs, a rocker, a love seat, or a chaise longue.

Other bedrooms were smaller and less decorated. The second-best bedroom was reserved for guests, because in those days long visits were common. When not occupied by a visitor, it might revert to an older child or be used as a sewing or art room.

The Bathroom Is Born
The most notable improvement in a few houses of the 1880s was the bathroom. Though not common in homes until after the turn of the century, bathrooms began to displace outhouses. Nonetheless, in most homes bedroom washstands and chamber pots continued to serve the functions that sinks and toilets do in today's bathrooms. Prior to the bathroom, some homes had "earth closets" where fresh soil was scattered to absorb and relieve the odors of body wastes. Though earth closets replaced chamber pots in some homes, cleaning the closets was still an unpleasant chore. Weekly visits were made by a public cart to remove "night soil."

A debate raged during this time about just how the bathroom should be decorated. One side called for it to be decorated just like any other room—with wallpaper,

Housing and Architecture 57

paneling, and cabinets to hide ugly plumbing. The opposition argued that this was extravagant and that such decorations were a dangerous breeding ground for germs and roaches, to say nothing of trapped gas. Tile and exposed plumbing were the alternative.

Those homes that did have a bathroom had only one. The fixtures were similar to today's—a porcelain basin, a "modern" flush toilet, and a bathtub. However, the tub was set on clawlike feet, and the bathroom pipes were generally exposed.

In the Future: Bathrooms without Bathtubs

Bathrooms in 2090 will not have a tub despite the fact that the room will be much larger than is true today. It will be a pleasant place where your grandchildren and great-grandchildren will spend lots of time. Instead of a tub there will be a shower where one will be surrounded by shower heads spraying water from all angles and providing a relaxing massage at the same time. Built-in soap and shampoo dispensers will be available within the shower. Those who want to soak and relax can step into a hot tub complete with a built-in whirlpool. With a turn of her head, your great-granddaughter will be able to reflect light from her eye to the light-sensitive switches on the television, stereo, and VCR built into the wall opposite the hot tub. Even a remote-control telephone will be available for those who like to talk to friends while relaxing in a hot tub.

Upon emerging from the hot tub, the bather will find moisturizers and skin oils available from automatic dispensers. A hair dryer, built into the wall, and a facial steamer, near a second sink below a fogproof mirror, will add to the joys of this fabulous room. Finally, a body analyzer, part of the continued movement toward better health by self-monitoring, will allow your future relatives to measure their weight, blood pressure, heart rate, blood sugar level, and the blood concentration of various other substances. Any irregularities will be cause for a change in diet or exercise, or a visit to a physician.

Other Rooms in the House of 2090

The formality of the American parlor of a century ago has disappeared. In today's larger home, the family room reflects the informality of modern living. This trend will continue. If any one thing will characterize the home of the future, it will be the computer—a relatively recent invention with a potential that we are just beginning to realize.

A century from now, if you were to knock on a friend's front door, the owner's voice incorporated into a computer program would greet you. When you responded, the voice of a frequent visitor, such as yourself, would be recognized by the computer and you would be invited in or asked to leave a message if your friend was not home. A visitor whose voice was unfamiliar to the computer would be asked to give his or her name and wait until the computer announced the visitor's presence to someone within. If no one was home, the computer would so inform the visitor. If a burglar attempted to break into an unoccupied house, the computer would set off an alarm announcing the intruder's presence to the neighborhood and to the police station.

Housing and Architecture

Each morning the master computer, controlling all household activities, would wake you, give you the latest news and weather report, remind you of your appointments for the day, and ask you what you'd like for breakfast. A robot, under the instruction of the central computer, would prepare your first meal of the day and have it ready when you entered the kitchen.

The central computer would regulate the temperature and humidity of each room. Heaters, air conditioners, dehumidifiers, humidifiers, fans, and windows will all be under its control. This will give you ideal conditions and the most efficient use of energy possible.

In dry weather, automatic sensors buried in the soil will detect its dryness and turn on an underground watering device. When the grass grows to a predetermined height, a robot will be directed to mow the lawn.

In addition to monitoring the house and lawn, the computer will serve as family secretary. It will not only take messages and inform callers of your whereabouts but will also process letters that you dictate while relaxing in the hot tub or a sauna adjacent to the bathroom.

Based on data collected by your body analyzer, the computer will see to it that robots prepare your meals with a balance of minerals, vitamins, and the basic foods that are just right for you. If medicines are required, the computer will order them from a pharmacy and be sure that they are presented to you at the proper time. (You'll still have to drink the water yourself.)

The family brain (computer) will be in daily contact with the bank to see that all bills are paid and that all monies paid to you are added to your account or used to automatically buy the securities you requested earlier.

In the evening you might watch a movie, listen to music, take a visual trip to some part of the world, or visit via videophone with a friend. All you need do is speak to the computer. It will recognize your voice, present a list of the films, trips, music, or phone numbers available, and let you select by touching your choice on its monitor.

Smaller homes, complete with built-in computers, will be built in factories and shipped for assembly on the owner's site. Many of these homes will be made of fiberglass (for strength) over Styrofoam (for insulation). An increasing number will take the form of geodesic domes—a shape that will be recognized by those who have visited the EPCOT Center at Walt Disney World Resort near Orlando, Florida.

A Variety of Homes

While most homes a century from now will probably be monitored by computers, the size and location of these homes will be even more varied than they are today. Some people will live in cities where skyscrapers will continue to be built. However, the mile-high buildings pictured by some futurists are unlikely. The cost and time involved in building such structures make it very difficult to attain financing.

Instead of reaching for the sky, more people will live underground or in homes with all but the south-facing windows buried in a hill. Since temperatures below ground remain quite constant, energy costs for heating and cooling such dwellings would be far less than they are for today's conventional buildings. Modern techniques for waterproofing and draining will make such

Housing and Architecture

homes more and more attractive as energy costs rise. However, if researchers find a way to control hydrogen fusion (the reaction that provides the energy of hydrogen bombs on earth and makes the stars glow in the heavens) within the next century, lower energy costs will reduce the demand for underground homes.

A century hence, there may even be a few homes beneath the sea. We know today that a battery connected to a submerged wire mesh frame will cause minerals in sea water to deposit on the wire. Once minerals begin to "grow" on the wire, shellfish attach themselves to the growing frame, providing a structure as strong as concrete. Such a structure, once enclosed, could be filled with air under pressure, making it a suitable place to live. The first such underwater buildings will serve as restaurants. People will enjoy the underwater view of sea life as they dine.

Since fish are known to be attracted to such underwater structures, some of these buildings will serve as homes for fish farmers. Later, when the safety of such structures has been established, larger underwater buildings will be grown along the coasts, and the people who live in them will commute to nearby cities through underwater tunnels.

In addition to underwater homes, floating villages will be built off the coast of southern cities. These floating towns will nurture and harvest shrimp, crabs, lobsters, and fish while providing energy to nearby cities. Flowing ocean water in the Gulf Stream and other ocean currents will power giant turbines beneath some of these floating villages. Generators connected to the turbines will provide electric power for nearby coastal cities. In some floating power stations, the energy to produce electricity will come from ocean thermal energy conversion (OTEC). On board yet other floating towns, giant windmills will convert the wind's energy to electricity.

Ocean waters off the coast of Florida and Hawaii are potential sites for OTEC. The temperature of the ocean at the surface may be 80 degrees Fahrenheit. Yet several thousand feet below, the water may be as cold as 40 degrees. A liquid with a low boiling point, such as ammonia, will boil in tubes resting in the ocean's surface water. This vapor will be used to turn the blades of turbines connected to electric generators. Exhaust vapors from the turbines will be cooled under pressure by cold water pumped from the ocean's depths, causing the vapor to condense. The liquid ammonia can then be recycled to pipes lying in the warm ocean surface so that the cycle may start again.

A Home in Space

So far, only a few astronauts and cosmonauts have spent time living in space, but a hundred years from now, space may be the only home thousands of people will know. If you were to visit a friend living in such a space home, you would have to reserve a seat aboard one of the fast shuttles making weekly trips between the earth and the space colony. As you approached your destination, you might see a giant wheel turning slowly in space. A reflection of your friend's hometown would be visible in a giant mirror above the colony. The mirror, lighting the interior of the space island, will be used to create night and day within the turning doughnut.

Housing and Architecture 63

This is a view of what an early space colony may look like. A central hub is connected to the ring or torus. The disc above the wheel, where an image of the colony can be seen, reflects sunlight into the living space within the torus. An area of photovoltaic cells between the spokes provides electric power.
Photo: NASA

THE FUTURE AND THE PAST 64

This view is from below the torus. It shows the lunar rocks that surround the colony and protect the inhabitants from cosmic rays. The long rectangle is a heat radiator attached to the original construction "shack" where people lived while building the colony. Below the colony, at the end of a long pole, is the manufacturing area where lunar ore will be processed. The sun, earth, and moon are in the background. Photo: NASA

The sphere in this photo will be more than 100 meters in diameter. It is the central hub of the space colony. The tower rising from the hub is where the docking ports for the space shuttles are located. The six spokes contain elevators leading from the hub to the torus where most of the space colonists live. The disc above the docks is the antenna used for communication with earth, other space colonies, and approaching space ships. Photo: NASA

THE FUTURE AND THE PAST

The giant wheel, about one mile in diameter, making one turn every minute, will create an artificial gravity similar to the kind you feel on some rides at an amusement park. Without artificial gravity, people in the space colony would be weightless. Experience has shown that muscles weaken and bones lose calcium in a weightless environment.

The outer surface of the wheel will be covered by rock-like debris—a waste slag produced at the colony's factory where moon ore is processed. The slag provides protection against cosmic rays and meteorites.

After your spaceship has docked at the central hub of the colony, you will enter an elevator. There you will be transported from the weightlessness at the hub's center to conditions similar to the earth's gravity at the outside of the giant wheel. As you walk toward the residential area of the colony, you will pass fields where crops grow and where goats, chickens, and rabbits can be seen within fenced enclosures. These plants and animals will provide food for the inhabitants of the space colony.

When you reach your friend's home, you find it to be a modular dwelling stacked on other similar structures, tastefully arranged to make the most of the very limited amount of space. Once inside, you will see that the houses are built on a frame of aluminum tubing. The covering attached to the frame is made of fireproof fiberglass. Through a window you can view a park where a pond surrounded by green grass and red flowers sparkles in sunlight as children play along its shore. As night falls, you are struck by the silence. Suddenly you realize there is no traffic in this island in space.

5

Work: Whatever Happened to the Iceman? And Would You Like to Drive a Space Tug?

> *When work is a pleasure, life is a joy!*
> *When work is duty, life is slavery.*
> —Makim Gorky, The Lower Depths

In 1890 most people in the United States worked on farms or in factories. The mechanization of farming during the twentieth century has reduced the number of farmers to a very small fraction of the nation's population. By 2090 the Information Age, which is dawning today, will reduce the number employed in factories as well. But the most dramatic change will be the return of the home as the work site for millions of Americans—a change that will be made possible by developments in computer and communications technology.

An Early View of Work

A nostalgic view of work in the early industrial period and on the old family farm collided with the efficient production required by the new industrialism of the 1880s and 1890s. For the worker, labor changed in a number of ways as the United States became the leading industrial country in the world. Most difficult for the workers to understand were the strict demands placed upon them by supervisors and foremen. The workers' reluctance to change their work habits and lose their independence was a problem of the age.

In the "old days," a man's labor was his own, and work and leisure were often combined. There was a flexibility to the work schedule that could not survive the modern industrial age. For example, what amounted to three-day weekends were not unusual for skilled craftsmen. "Blue Mondays" were lost production days as workers recovered from weekend partying. In some trades, "Saint Mondays" were considered holidays, and Labor Day was established on Monday as a remembrance of those times. By an informal agreement among themselves, craftsmen limited their production to keep prices high.

Agricultural work was just as flexible. It really did not matter when a job was finished as long as it was done before the next season. When a farmer found time for a breather, he stopped and relaxed. If he was bored, he moved to another task. Both farm and factory workers labored hard for a while and then took time to celebrate. One celebration of this sort was the first Thanksgiving Day, which was a harvest feast.

A Change in the Nature of Work

Such informal work habits could not be permitted in a modern industrial society. Workers were not used to the pace, effort, and strain of production as machines got bigger, faster, and more dangerous.

Many workers must have been unhappy in their jobs and felt the only good thing about work was the money, which they could spend to improve their lives. Even the money was not impressive, however. After working from fifty-five to sixty hours a week, an unskilled laborer earned about $1.25 a day. His skilled co-worker received about double that wage. The average yearly income for a factory worker in 1890 was only $486. However, prices in 1890 were much lower than they are today. (See Table 1.)

Accidents were a regular occurrence. Because there were no government regulations or inspections of the workplace, many worked in unhealthful and unsafe conditions. The United States had the highest industrial accident rate in the world. There was no workers' compensation for disability or injuries. People had to work to get paid and therefore often returned to work before they were fully recovered. Similarly, there were no pensions, so older workers stayed on doing lighter jobs for a few cents an hour for as long as they could. Even the miseries of factory work were better than unemployment, which meant financial ruin.

Nonetheless, factory owners demanded more production, better quality goods, and increased worker efficiency. They tried a number of ways to reach these goals. "Speedups" were a common method. A machine was speeded up, or a "rabbit"—a model worker hired at a special wage—was paid to perform faster than those around him. On the one hand, the machine determined the speed of work and paced the laborer. On the other, the workers had to keep up with the rabbit or lose their jobs. Workers disliked being controlled by the boss's machines or henchmen, and they resented the loss of independence in making decisions related to their jobs.

The workers' independence was further sacrificed in "time and motion studies," begun in the 1880s and 1890s. Pioneered by Frederick W. Taylor, the originator of Taylorism, or scientific management, these studies called for an engineer with a stopwatch to measure precisely how long it took to complete each step in a job and establish a standard time for that assignment. A worker was expected to maintain the set time or be fired. He or she received a higher wage for consistently doing a task in less than the standard time. Mass production was divided into small, specialized tasks. Workers felt belittled. They were no longer craftspeople paid for doing quality work; they were just laborers who were paid for robotlike time on the job. Mass production had been introduced into some factories making guns as early as the Civil War. Henry Ford's assembly line, designed to produce his Model T car (1913), was the height of this type of industrial efficiency.

In some factories workers were paid for piecework—that is, they were paid only for what they made. To earn extra money the worker was required to make more products. Urban workers in dingy factories could recall that at the end of a day's work on a farm, they could still relax and enjoy nature. By the turn of the century those days were but dim memories.

The middle-class white-collar worker was not free from the tension of the workplace either. Being a businessperson now had little to do with ownership. In many cases he or she worked for a large corporation, which raised a number of questions. How much work was enough? Could an employee work too much? Both in the office and on the factory floor, people were concerned about the impersonality of the new corporation. There was no direct contact with owners, who once knew their workers well. The individual no longer seemed important. A worker who was sick or injured could be readily replaced.

Workers developed a number of strategies to cope with these terrible working conditions. Quitting was the easiest solution. But older workers and family men could ill afford to lose their only source of income. Absenteeism was another means of silent protest, but a worker who missed too many days would be labeled unreliable or uncooperative, which could lead to dismissal. Picketing (marching in front of a business with signs charging the employer with unfair practices), boycotting (refusing to buy the company's goods), and striking (refusing to work) were other alternatives for the workers.

As industry grew bigger, laborers began to organize. The turning point in labor organization came in 1881 with the establishment of the American Federation of Labor (AFL). The architect of the organization was a New York City cigarmaker, Samuel Gompers, who served as president of the AFL for forty years. Gompers realized that laborers had to take work as it was and not what they felt it should be. Technology, management techniques, and employers' rejection of traditional work habits were not going to change, so Gompers focused on winning higher wages, reduced working hours, and better conditions. Unions sought not to change the nature of work but to limit it by shortening the workweek and improving safety conditions.

During the period from 1881 to 1900, workers voiced their dissatisfaction by using their strongest weapon—the strike—more than two thousand times. Strikes were very violent in the 1890s, when the country was racked by the worst depression in its history up to that time. (A depression occurs when the amount of buying and selling declines. During a depression there is rising unemployment and falling profits, production, and sales.) With few exceptions the unions lost. Employers blamed the strikes not on poor working conditions but on conspiracies meant to destroy the industrial might of the country. Unfortunately for the workers, the authorities sided with management.

Women and Work

Women as well as men fought for change in the workplace and received national attention with the establishment of a women's division of the Knights of Labor, an early labor union that preceded the AFL. Leona Barry was the guiding force in this women's movement. She served four years as an investigator assigned to educate the public about the needs of female laborers. Another legendary union woman was Mary Harris—known as Mother Jones—who aggressively sought to organize the nation's miners.

The AFL was an all-male organization. The men justified their position by arguing that women should stay at home and not take jobs away from men. In 1903 the Women's Trade Union League was founded by Mary O'Sullivan. The league was interested in uniting women, but its other goals were basically the same as those of the AFL. These women also wanted to acquaint the nation with the abuse of women in home industries and sweatshops—small unhealthy, unsafe, low-paying factories usually associated with the garment industry.

Most jobs for women were performed by single working-class women between sixteen and twenty-four years of age. Middle-class women seldom worked for money outside the home. As a rule, married women did not work unless their husbands were unemployed or unable to hold a job because of injury, drunkenness, or some other problem. Since women were considered the weaker sex, it stood to reason they could not hold "men's jobs" and certainly should not get as much pay. Job competition between the sexes, so feared by the early AFL, never really materialized. Women were given only subordinate and low-paying jobs.

The nineteenth-century notion of the "proper" role for women was reflected in their employment as domestic servants, maids, cooks, or laundresses. By 1890, as new jobs opened up, however, fewer women were willing to take these menial positions. Instead, they moved into clerical and other "white blouse" positions. The invention of the typewriter (1867), cash register (1879), and adding machine (1891) simplified office and sales work. Companies were willing to hire young women for these jobs. High schools provided most of the necessary vocational training, but industry still viewed these positions as unskilled and therefore paid the women lower wages.

Three areas of employment with higher social acceptance for women became popular during the era—teaching, nursing, and social work. Such opportunities made employment for middle-class women more acceptable. Some women became "blue blouse" workers for industry, but as always, their wages were lower than men's. Women were most visible in the garment and textile industries, and they held some positions in other industries as packers, inspectors, or assemblers.

Women workers did differ from men in important ways. First, few women worked for more than ten years. Work never became a major part of their lives because society decreed that family and children should be far more important. Second, women were less likely to unionize and strike. There were important exceptions to this, such as the shirtwaist-workers' strikes in New York City, which were led by women.

On the surface, labor improvements for women seemed small indeed. However, increased employment opportunities made women more independent and gave them a much more public role and character than they had enjoyed earlier. This preparation period led to increasingly outspoken demands for women's voting rights in the early part of the twentieth century.

Police as Professionals

The development of professional police forces took place during this era. Prior to 1880 people had little confidence in law-enforcement officers, who were often incorrectly referred to as peace officers. Toughness and street savvy were the main qualifications for becoming a peace officer. These patrolmen were certainly not students of constitutional rights; police brutality was common. Officers often took bribes or received their appointments to the force as a payback for political favors. Police, in general, were not respected or supported by many citizens.

During the last two decades of the nineteenth century, however, the pleas of reformers and a growing national concern about lawlessness led to change. Civil service examinations replaced political favoritism as the pathway to becoming a law-enforcement officer. As police became more effective and honest, they gained public support and respect. The idea of police as professionals became accepted as the nation entered the twentieth century.

Child Labor

In 1900, over one million children under age sixteen worked in the nation's industries. There was no separation of work and childhood for the laboring class. Children learned about factory life at an early age by hearing their parents' stories, living close to factories, and running errands to the workshops, such as taking lunch to their fathers. They were also aware that the family counted on their contribution at the earliest possible time. The most financially successful families were those that had at least one child working. The most vulnerable families were those with infants and older couples with no children to help them out.

Work began at an early age, usually fourteen, though

some children as young as three performed agricultural piecework, such as sorting tobacco leaves. Enforcement of minimum-age laws was very lax and children often lied about their age. It was not uncommon for twelve-year-olds to hold industrial jobs. Usually children got their positions through the influence of a relative. Once they were hired, this same relative, in an informal family apprenticeship, taught the new employee his or her job.

Children viewed their employment as a symbol of adulthood. There was an accompanying sense of independence. Nevertheless, most children turned over all their pay to their parents. In praising the value of child labor, business reinforced the idea that working led to maturity, independence, and an education that schools could not provide. Businessmen felt they were doing the public a service by hiring youngsters. Everyone knew that unemployed children, especially poor boys, were a threat to the peace of the neighborhood. Work kept youth gainfully occupied. Where unions were strong, it was tough for children to find work. But this only forced boys into nonunion jobs that were often unsafe and unhealthy as well as low-paying.

If there was education in work, most child workers missed it. Conditions were deplorable. No special considerations were given to children because of their age. They worked in the same environment and faced the same hazards as adults. "Breaker boys" straddled a conveyor belt and picked waste rock from freshly mined coal. The fact that they breathed coal dust and frequently cut their hands was of no concern to their foremen, who would fire them if they left the job site to seek relief. In glass

A young girl working in a cotton mill in about 1900. Photo: UPI/Bettmann Newsphotos

factories, children worked from five in the evening to three in the morning, bringing molten glass to molders. The work was considered too hot for adults. Children who worked in textile mills in the South sometimes fell asleep when they worked the night shift. Foremen doused them with cold water to keep them alert. In a Chicago caramel factory six stories high, there was no fire escape and only wooden stairs as a way to the ground. During the Christmas season when candy was selling well, children worked eighty-four hours a week, toiling each day from 7:00 A.M. to 9:00 P.M.

Government, for the most part, ignored child labor abuse. It wasn't until private individuals and organiza-

THE FUTURE AND THE PAST 78

tions, like Lewis Hine and the National Child Labor Committee (1904), took a stand that the country reacted. Even so, it was not until the 1940s that child labor laws became effective. It was ironic that child labor abuse was rampant in a nation that had been so child-centered in 1890. Child labor in the United States was the country's shame.

More Changes in the World of Work

In 1890, work, to most people, meant farming or a job in a factory. Today there is a greater variety of employment, and many jobs that were common a century ago or less have disappeared or soon will. Gone is the iceman and gone are the iceboxes he filled. Gone, too, is the harness maker, the milkman, the pin setter in bowling alleys, and the livery stable. In rapid decline are jobs for elevator operators, coal miners, meter readers, and factory workers. And a century from now it is likely that secretaries, teachers, mail clerks, and mail carriers, at least in the way that we know their jobs today, will have disappeared.

As old jobs fade from view, new ones are continually being created. In 1945, at the end of World War II, astronauts, word processors, computer programmers, and nuclear engineers were unknown. And only a decade ago no one would have contemplated a career in CAT (computed axial tomography) or PET (positron emission tomography). Yet, CAT scans and PET scans are common in hospitals today.

As the United States changes from heavy industry to high technology and information-centered companies, opportunities for employment in new areas continue to grow. Today many young people seek training in electronics, fiber optics, data processing, molecular biology, ecology, space technology, and genetic engineering. Tomorrow we predict a growing need for people trained in many new fields. These include information technology, sea mining, OTEC, holography, robot technology, waste management, fusion engineering—in which electricity will be produced by the fusion of hydrogen atoms—and other kinds of employment that we cannot foresee. After all, who would have imagined a career in computer technology a century ago?

One of the major changes in all occupations will be from a vertical chain of command to a horizontal arrangement. Instead of a person in authority making a decision and then telling others what to do, decisions will be made by consensus. A number of people will be consulted, and discussions will be held before people finally decide what to do. The reason for such a change stems from the fact that most people will be well educated and will be able to think rationally and objectively about questions related to their vocation. Consequently, their thoughts and ideas will be both valuable and valued.

Jobs in the Information Age

We are living at the beginning of the Information Age. With computers that can process, store, sort, arrange, and retrieve information quickly and efficiently, we have at our fingertips vast amounts of information on virtually any subject. The collection, management, and sale of that information will provide jobs for millions over the next century.

The development of software to store knowledge gleaned through research and to transfer information from libraries to computer screens or printers is already in full swing. By 2090, word processing, electronic filing, electronic mail (computer to computer through telephone lines), and computers that will transfer the spoken word to the printed page and the screen will eliminate the need for secretaries, mail clerks, and letter carriers. There will be postal service for packages, but all correspondence will be done through computers. You'll be able to buy special software that will intercept and destroy electronic junk mail.

A Longer Life in a New World

In 1850 the average American could expect to live to age thirty-nine. By 1950 life expectancy had increased to sixty-nine years. With improved medical knowledge and greater individual attention to personal health, the life expectancy for those born in 2090 will probably be about one hundred years. The combination of longer life and the likelihood that changes in job types will continue to accelerate means that many people will change occupations during their lifetimes. The process of changing jobs or professions will be made easier by computer simulations that will provide realistic settings for everything from flying a spaceship to doing brain surgery.

Conducting Business in a Moneyless Society

Computer connections between banks, businesses, and citizens will eliminate the need for money. You will pay

Work

your bills by transferring credit from your bank account to your merchant's account. Statements, balances, checking, and all other banking operations will be done on computer through connections between banks, companies, and consumers.

Banks will offer financial management services that will allow you to obtain investment and tax information on your computer screen. From a menu you'll be able to analyze your financial portfolio and choose where and how to invest your money. Coins and paper money now used for buying tokens, tickets, newspapers, and other small items will be done by means of a credit card that you will simply hold under a laser device. Your Social Security number will be read by the laser, and the "money" will be transferred from your account to the proper theater, newsstand, and so forth.

Automated production lines and computer connections will allow production on demand. Companies will keep minimum stockpiles because direct sales between producer and consumer will eliminate retail sales. You'll be able to order your new electric car directly from Detroit after doing comparative shopping on your computer-controlled television channels. Similarly, you'll be able to choose the site of your next vacation after viewing different vacation sites on television or taking a simulated trip to the site through integrated video-computer-television programs.

Disappearing Resources

Pollution, dwindling resources, and questions of waste disposal have led us to realize that the notion that humans can conquer nature, which was prominent a century ago, was a dangerous one. During the next century, the realization that the human species must blend with, not compete with, nature will be not only recognized but practiced.

Today we recycle about 25 percent of the iron, aluminum, and paper we produce. In the future, we will recycle a considerably larger fraction of these and other materials. Since it requires twenty times as much energy to extract aluminum from ores as it does to recycle the metal, it is clear that the high cost of energy early in the next century will strongly encourage recycling.

A number of approaches will be used to solve the problem of the world's diminishing supply of natural resources such as fossil fuels and metals. To avoid burying ourselves in our own trash, as well as to conserve the resources we have, we will separate and recycle metal cans and other metal products, paper, glass, plastics, garbage, and other materials. Reverse vending machines will return the deposit you paid on a can when you return the can to such a machine. Combustible trash will serve as a fuel in generating electric power. Genetic engineers will develop microorganisms that will degrade plastics, clean up oil spills, extract metals from ores, and produce hydrogen from water. Initially, the hydrogen will be used as a fuel to reduce our dependence on fossil fuels. Later, the hydrogen will be separated, and the less abundant isotopes will be used to fuel the fusion reactors that will provide an increasing amount of electric power in 2090.

Genetic engineers will also develop plants that will supply the oil needed to replace that which is currently being pumped from the earth. And industrial engineers will develop plastics and ceramic materials that are stronger and lighter than the metals they will replace.

To further supplement our supply of minerals, we will establish mines on the moon. Lunar soil will be vaporized and ionized by concentrating the sun's energy in a solar furnace. The ionized vapor, propelled through magnetic fields produced from electric currents in superconducting wires, will separate into elements—metals and otherwise—present in the lunar rocks. Some of the elements will be shuttled back to earth, and some will be processed in space factories that probably will be in an experimental stage in 2090. By the twenty-second century, most of the lunar products will be used in space factories to avoid the high cost of sending space shuttles from earth to lunar orbit. And by that time, space tugs powered by solar sails or fusion engines will begin hauling asteroids to space factories. There, the metals, carbon, nitrogen, and hydrogen in the asteroids will be extracted.

6

Clothing and Fashion: Our Ever-Changing View of What the Well-Dressed Person Should Wear

Every generation laughs at the old fashions, but follows religiously the new.
—Henry David Thoreau, Walden, Or Life in the Woods

By today's standards, the fashions of the last decade of the nineteenth century appear to have been torturously uncomfortable, and the most excruciating punishment was reserved for women. Men, but especially women, were covered by yards of material, and their movements were confined by high starched collars, corsets, and long, tight-fitting underwear.

The more casual and comfortable clothing of today will continue to be worn through the next century. It is likely that the present tendency of men and women to wear similar clothing will lead to dress of an even more unisex nature by 2090.

Your Ancestors' Underwear

Beginning in the 1870s, it was a widely accepted notion that wearing plant fibers next to the skin was unhealthful, since they did not absorb body fluids. As a result, long, itchy woolen underwear was standard for both sexes. Underwear came in two styles: separates—a long-sleeved shirt and ankle-length drawers; or the popular union suit, a long one-piece garment that buttoned up the front and had a drop seat.

Mercifully, cotton-knit underwear later replaced wool. Yet even these garments were tight-fitting and often were fleece-lined, like today's sweat shirts. With a growing demand for comfort, men's B.V.D.'s (named for the manufacturer) came into vogue. These were knee-length, loose-fitting, sleeveless cotton union suits.

Women's undergarments became more comfortable as well. A sleeveless, calf-length cotton or linen chemise, the forerunner of the modern slip, became popular, as did underdrawers similar to today's culottes. These two garments constituted a type of feminine union suit.

Men's Fashions

Men's fashions were less troublesome than women's and did not change significantly during this period. The well-dressed gentleman of the 1880s could stride into the turn of the century virtually unnoticed. In fact, men of the 1880s dressed quite like men today, except for a few details.

The short suit coat, first seen in the 1850s, was popular in the 1870s and readily accepted in 1880. It was a high-

A formal picture of the time. Note the detachable collar and the high-buttoned coat. Photo: Courtesy Scoville Library

buttoned coat, the top button of which was at collarbone level. There was no difference in seasonal wear. The blue wool suit favored by most men was worn winter and summer.

Shirts were pullovers with only a couple of buttons down the front. (Shirts that opened like a coat did not

Two dapper young gentlemen of the 1880s posed for a formal photograph. Notice the derby, the high shoes, the high-buttoned coat, and the detachable collars. Photo: Courtesy Scoville Library

become popular until the 1920s.) Called neckband shirts, they had no collars and no cuffs. Detachable collars and cuffs allowed for more wear in the days before washing machines. Collars ranged from an inch and a half to three inches in height and had to be changed daily. They were made of linen and stiffly starched. The combination of starch and height often made it difficult for a man to turn his head. The constant need for freshly washed and starched collars and cuffs gave men a cause for concern, not to mention the work it caused their wives. In an effort to ease the burden of laundering, some collars were made of paper or celluloid, a type of plastic that could be wiped clean. Sadly, for smokers, these had a tendency to catch fire. They were also considered less fashionable than linen, which remained the preferred material. Most mail-order catalogs had a large section devoted to the sale of collars for as little as a dollar a dozen. No gentleman would be seen in public without a collar and a necktie to hide his collar button.

Men's trousers have changed very little over the years, although it was the turn of the century before cuffs, creases, and belts became popular. Your great-great grandfather wore suspenders. Men regularly wore ankle-high tie or buttoned-up boots until the 1920s when oxfords became fashionable.

Today the United States is a hatless society, even on the coldest days, but to go bareheaded a century ago was not considered proper. Hat styles varied from the cloth cap worn by workers and sportsmen to cowboy-type hats. The last word in style was the bowler—or derby, as it was more frequently called. The top hat was also popular.

These styles gave way in the summertime to the boater, a stiff straw hat decorated with a bright band.

Laborers generally wore the neckband shirt without a collar in warm weather. In cooler weather they preferred a flannel shirt with a turn-down collar similar to today's. In the East, some workers wore big overalls made of blue denim. These were developed in the 1870s by James Orr and his partners under the Sweet-Orr label. Similar overalls are still available today.

Out West, Levi Strauss was already selling pants with distinctive copper-riveted pockets. He first used tent canvas, probably tan in color, to supply California gold rush miners with durable, heavy-duty pants. As early as the 1880s, your great-great grandparents would have been familiar with blue jeans.

Women's Fashions

Women's fashions did not share the stability of men's. Their clothes were always changing, based on the latest creations from Paris, London, and Berlin. Late nineteenth-century fashion hid women's figures by enveloping them in yards of material from the neck to feet. High, upright choker collars, customarily trimmed with lace, were common. Women of this era pioneered the layered look. Fashion in the 1880s demanded an overdress and underdress of two different materials. Women favored gowns made of brown, red, and green silk or velvet and elaborately trimmed with lace, ribbon, or fringe. Your great-great grandmother's dress and petticoats, together, weighed between ten and thirty pounds!

Formal attire of the 1880s, a high-collared, "tied back" dress with bustle. Photo: Courtesy Scoville Library

Clothing and Fashion

In the 1880s, the bulk of the hoopskirt of the post-Civil War period was pushed to the back of the skirt. The style was called the "tied-back" look. Dresses were drawn so tightly over the knees that women found it difficult to walk. The bustle, which was out of style in the late 1870s, later found its way back into women's wardrobes. This was a separate garment that made the back of a woman's dress bulge out. One kind of bustle was made of metal rods and looked like a bird cage tied about the waist. Later, the bustle became a pad of steel and cotton, or horsehair, attached by hooks to the waistband.

Dresses also had a "brush binding" of less expensive material around the hem. Since dresses were floor length, they brushed the ground and got dirty and torn, so the brush binding had to be replaced regularly. Essentially, a woman had only one free hand, since the other was always occupied with lifting the hem of her dress off the ground. In the late 1880s, hemlines rose to above the ankle, only to drop again in the 1890s.

The feminine ideal of the eighties and nineties was a tall woman with an hourglass figure. Eighteen to twenty-one inches was considered the ideal waist size. A man's hands were supposed to be able to circle a woman's waist. To achieve this goal, women wore tight corsets, which supposedly had a practical purpose as well. Since women were considered weak and fragile, the corset was believed to serve as a brace. It was made of cotton with stiff wire or baleen (whalebone) supports sewn between the layers. Generally it hooked in the front and could be tightened around a woman's waist by means of laces in the back. Physicians warned women of the physical dangers of tight corseting, which not uncommonly caused broken ribs or collapsed lungs. Because the corset made taking a deep breath impossible, fainting was another common occurrence—one that unfortunately added to the stereotypical view of women as the weaker sex.

The small dainty feminine craze extended to women's

The advertising caption that accompanied these two drawings of corsets read: "The boning of these corsets throughout is of duplex, coated, rust-proof, finest quality watch-spring steel wire, thoroughly covered by a patented rubber and muslin covering, and absolutely guaranteed not to rust or discolor—moreover, unbreakable and lasting to the highest degree."
Photos: Courtesy Scoville Library

Clothing and Fashion

shoes. The "toothpick" shoe, which was very narrow, with a pointed toe, and a one- to two-inch heel, was all the rage one hundred years ago. Like men's footwear, it was an over-the-ankle boot that laced or buttoned. Some women cramped their feet by wearing shoes that were too small to achieve the desired small foot look. Standing in place was extremely painful, walking was difficult, and running was impossible.

In the 1890s, with increased female participation in sports like tennis, golf, and cycling, and with more women working in business offices, there began a significant change in apparel. The more active life replaced croquet and teas and helped to lessen the notion that women were

A group of women attired in fashions of the time. Notice the woman in the middle with the bow tie is wearing a shirtwaist.
Photo: Courtesy Scoville Library

fragile. This led to a demand for simpler, more comfortable clothing that allowed ease of motion.

From this change emerged the shirtwaist, or blouse. Very simple in form, these were easily produced, available in large quantities at moderate prices, and provided variety in the wardrobe. At first they were white linen or cotton with the familiar high collar, but soon plaid blouses and fashionable shirtwaists made of silk and velvet and decorated with ribbon became popular. Skirts changed as well, moving to a less restrictive A-line style that remained ankle length until the late 1890s. The shirtwaist, along with a dark-toned A-line skirt and a jacket, combined to create the tailored suit for women. The modern version of this is a main part of any businesswoman's wardrobe today.

We don't know as much about the everyday wear of the homemaker or working-class woman, since few of these garments survived. Customarily, these workday dresses were worn for as long a time as possible and then cut down for children or torn up into rags or pieces for quilts. Certainly the everyday corset had to be looser to allow women to work in reasonable comfort. Workday dresses were similar in style to "dressy" dresses but looser and simpler. Less material was used, so they were lighter as well.

Children's Fashions

All toddlers wore white linen or cotton smocks until just before they started school. At school age, girls began to wear flat-heeled shoes and dresses patterned after their

A boy dressed in a Buster Brown suit. Photo: Courtesy Scoville Library

mothers' but lighter in weight and of ankle length, to allow them to play. Tiny corsets were available for girls as young as three or four, but most girls didn't wear them.

Boys and girls shared one outfit that remained popular well into the twentieth century—the sailor suit. This year-round favorite was linen or flannel in the summer and wool in the winter. The girl's version had a kilted skirt.

A popular style for boys was based on the 1886 publication of *Little Lord Fauntleroy*. The book set off a fashion craze for the Fauntleroy suit—a black or deep blue velvet jacket and shorts with a satin sash, knee socks, and a white shirt with a large lace collar. Later the Buster Brown outfit became popular. In place of the velvet and the lace collar, this suit had a wool jacket and a wide starched collar. It was always worn with a large black silk scarf tied in a bow. Both suits were considered "sissy outfits." We can only guess at the number of arguments they caused between reluctant sons and their persistent mothers.

Even after escaping these suits, a youth was still condemned to short pants. At about age eight, he began to wear knickers, pants cut just below the knee. These were worn through the grammar school years. Only as an adolescent did a young man begin to dress like his father. Long pants for younger boys did not become accepted until the 1940s. Prior to that, boys wore shorts or knickers.

The Clothes of Tomorrow

The trend to less formal dress has already begun. A generation ago, one seldom saw a man without a coat and

Clothing and Fashion

tie or a woman dressed in jeans dining in a restaurant. Today, informal attire in restaurants, churches, theaters, and business is not uncommon.

A century from now, formal dress will be seen only at weddings, funerals, and parties sponsored by the very wealthy. In a few families, where tradition is treasured, formal dress at dinners, dances, and church services will be retained, but in general, dress will be even less formal than it is today.

Since many more people will be working at home, they will not wear suits or dresses to work. Once that pattern is established, people will not dress up even when they meet with others.

In schools the present trend to informal dress will continue. Children used to dressing casually at home will not don formal clothes to meet their peers when they go to school.

Since special occasions will be rare, formal clothing will seldom be seen. As a result it will remain very similar to what it is today. Informal clothing, on the other hand, will vary tremendously depending on the season, geographical location, and individual taste. You can be sure that clothing designers will spend more time creating appealing casual wear than formal apparel.

Finally, the current trend to reduce the differences between the clothing worn by men and women will continue. A century from now boys and girls and men and women will wear virtually the same clothes.

7

Communication: From the Telegraph to Intergalactic Messages

The wave of the future is coming and there is no fighting it.
—Ann Morrow Lindbergh, The Wave of the Future

Though the telegraph brought an end to the pony express, thus closing a chapter of the Old West, the telephone, invented in 1876, made long-distance communication far more personal. Today we have computerized and "smart" telephones. We also have radio, television, and satellite systems that enable us to send both messages and pictures around the world and into space. A century from now the union of computer, telephone, and television, using fiber optics technology, will lead to vastly improved methods of communication. Improvements in communication will bring about dramatic changes in our entire social structure—particularly in education and transportation.

In a period characterized by change, communications remained stable through the last two decades of the nineteenth century. The telegraph and the telephone were well established by the 1880s. After a great deal of legal controversy, artist-turned-inventor Samuel F.B. Morse was recognized as the inventor of the telegraph and was issued a patent in 1844. By 1861, in time for the Civil War, telegraph lines reached across the country. The major accomplishment in telegraphy, after Morse, was the work of Cyrus Field who dedicated his life and fortune to developing the transatlantic cable. The *Great Eastern*, the largest ship ever built, until the *Lusitania*, successfully completed laying the cable in 1866.

Alexander Graham Bell, an immigrant Scot who became a U.S. citizen in 1882, invented the telephone in 1876. Bell was neither a mechanical expert nor an engineer; he was a speech teacher for the deaf in Boston. The telephone was a result of his efforts to aid the hearing impared, especially his wife, who was deaf from birth, using electricity to make sounds. The first telephone message—"Mr. Watson, come here. I want you"—was accidental. Bell had spilled battery acid on his pants and needed his assistant's help. In 1880 there was one phone for every thousand Americans. Within twenty years there was one phone for every seventeen Americans. The rapid spread of the telephone dramatically improved by Thomas Edison, made a vast change in long distance communication.

In 1895 the world saw the first hint of what was to come in communication when twenty-one-year-old Guglielmo Marconi invented the wireless, or radio. Marconi sent messages a distance of one mile without benefit of wires or cable. But it was not until 1920 that radio was established in the United States. In that year station KDKA in Pittsburgh began regular broadcasting by announcing the presidential election returns.

Today's Smart Phones

Though the basic technology of the telephone has not changed much in the last century, we've come a long way from the old crank phones to the touch dialing of today. People who own so-called smart phones are able to transfer a call to another number or to keep trying a busy number without redialing. Some smart phones display the number of the caller when your phone rings. If it's your friend, you'll probably answer. But if it's someone trying to sell you a magazine you don't need, you'll let it ring. There are even phone systems that allow you to record a message, store it, and then automatically call a series of numbers at designated times, deliver the message, and record the party's responses. A person in business can set up such a program, go play golf or tennis for three hours, and return to review the responses of those who were called. Of course, other business persons with similar systems may be doing the same thing so that the most common response might be, "Please leave your message and I'll get back to you as soon as possible."

While such modern telephones were never envisioned by Alexander Graham Bell, they will be viewed as rather primitive a century from now.

Communication: The Key to the Future

More than any other factor, developments in communication technology will generate the changes of the future. We have already seen how the declining cost of communication, together with increasing transportation costs caused by the growing scarcity of fuels, will lead many to work at home. This change in the nation's work habits will, in turn, alter family life and reintroduce the old sense of community or neighborhood.

Modern digital transmitters and receivers convert sounds and pictures to the on-off, or 1-and-0 signals that form the basis of computer technology. These signals, like the varying electric currents used to transmit most of today's telephone messages, can be sent along telephone wires. But digital signals eliminate the static, fading, and background noise that sometimes interfere with telephone calls. A century from now most signals will probably be digital. They will be sent as light pulses along glass fibers, not as changing electric currents along copper wires. The energy requirements for sending digital signals on glass fibers is only 0.1 percent of that for sending varying electric currents on copper wires. To carry 36,000 simultaneous telephone conversations using digital signals on glass fibers would require only 24 strands of glass, forming a cable about as thick as your finger. To carry the same number of telephone conversations with the technology commonly in use today requires 3,600 strands of copper wire with a total diameter of about three inches.

The capacity of glass fibers to carry large numbers of signals simultaneously will make videotelephones and videoteleconferencing possible. In 2090 seeing as well as hearing the person you call will be part of every phone call. Small group conferences will be conducted on a face-to-face basis through televideo conferences. Such systems will drastically reduce the need for travel and will allow more and more people to work at home.

If you visit the Horizons exhibit in EPCOT Center at

Walt Disney World Resort near Orlando, Florida, you'll see what a videotelephone might look like in tomorrow's living room. In one of the Communicore exhibits in EPCOT Center you'll see how, in the future, a phone dial will put you in contact with various specialized television channels for world news, local news, weather, financial reports, sports, and so forth.

By dialing a particular channel, future shoppers will be able to see televised Yellow Pages where information about purchasing most items will be available. By calling various manufacturers of the item on their videophones they'll be able to do comparative shopping while sitting in their own living rooms. Similarly, views of vacation sites as well as simulated tours of those places will be possible by interactive telephone, television, and video.

Comptelvideo

Comptelvideo—the union of television, telephone, video, and computer—will enable people in the future to correspond through electronic mail as well as by videophone. You'll obtain most of your mail, not through your mailbox, but through your computer. There will be stored messages from friends, family, and colleagues with whom you are working, and responses to requests for information that you sent to other people. Part of your day will be spent responding to your mail. Your responses, which will be translated from your dictation to your computer's screen and memory, will be stored in your electronic file and sent through a modem and telephone lines to the recipients of your comments. Of course, if you feel the need to discuss something face-to-face, you can always use your videophone.

Satcomptelvideo

In addition to translating your voice into print, future combined communication systems, called satcomptelvideos, will be able to translate a message from one language into another and then put it into a translated voice as well as print and send the message across the earth. For example, suppose you are an American international business person engaged in a televideo conference with people from Japan, Germany, the Soviet Union, and Italy. Communication satellites allow television and telephone signals to be sent from continent to continent in a matter of tenths of a second. You will receive the telephone portion of the signals via satellite through your computer translating program. The words spoken in German, Russian, Italian, and Japanese will automatically be translated into English. Similarly, your statements and questions will be translated into other languages for your listeners.

Computer translating programs will eliminate the demand for an international language. Through the marvels of computer programming, people will be able to speak their native tongue and still be understood by others who cannot speak or understand that language. Such programs will help bring the world closer together and enhance the exchange of ideas at an international level.

The interaction of computers and satellites will allow those traveling in automobiles to view their position on a map. The map of the particular locality will be seen on a screen on the dashboard of their car. By pressing a button the driver will be able to view an enlargement of the area through which the car is moving. Such a picture will reveal the names of local streets. Pressing another button will add arrows to the map that will indicate the best route through the locality.

Drivers and pedestrians as well might be wearing miniature telephones (Dick Tracy wrist radios). These devices will enable people to communicate, through satellite telephone, with police, fire departments, ambulance services, and other emergency agencies as well as with business associates and personal friends.

Advances in communication technology will make comptelvideo banking, investing, shopping, conferencing, and entertainment common a century from now. Future citizens may even enjoy televoting. Instead of making a journey to the polls, they will dial a number to place the names of candidates on their computer monitor. By touching the names of the candidates they prefer, they will cast their ballot.

Communication and Crime

Advances in communication technology will affect crime prevention, crime detection, prosecution, and the nature of prisons. Though we would all like to see an end to crime in the future, such a complete change is unlikely. However, we may well see a reduction in crime. An older population will tend to reduce the percentage of the population engaged in crime. Statistics show that it is younger people who are more likely to commit crimes. Since more parents will work at home, they will be in a position to exercise greater control over their children. With closer parental supervision, fewer children and young adults will engage in criminal behavior. In addition, both businesses and homes will have better computerized security systems. These systems will be in direct communication with local police or neighborhood patrols. Finally, a moneyless society should put muggers out of business.

A computer communication network, to which each local police department will have access, will provide a national data bank on all felons. In addition to fingerprints and other identifying information, the data on criminals will include photographs and voice prints. A voice print is a record of the sound waves produced when someone talks. Since each person has a characteristic voice print, these prints will be as important as fingerprints in identifying criminals. In fact, instead of wiretaps police may use small computer chips attached to a suspect's clothing. The chips will broadcast the speaker's voice to a computer located in police headquarters.

By using laser light beams investigators will be able to detect fingerprints on the bodies of murder victims. The light will cause certain chemicals in the thin film of the print to fluoresce. Continued advances in the analysis of the genetic materials (DNA analysis) found in living cells will enable detectives to identify suspects from small samples of blood or semen. Computer graphics programs will allow a forensic scientist to enter measurements of a victim's skull into a computer. The scientist will then be able to obtain a detailed picture of what that person looked like.

The time delays in bringing a case to trial will diminish as new computer software is developed to streamline the legal process. This software of the future will allow lawyers to search a legal data base for precedents. The software will also enable lawyers to chart, organize, and present evidence, and compile testimony from experts. For trial purposes, the forensic scientists, psychiatrists, doctors, and researchers will not have to report to court to be examined by the prosecution and defense. Through comptelvideo they can be "in court" while seated in their labs or offices.

Those convicted of crime will seldom go to the kinds of prisons we know today. Many minor crimes will be punished by making those convicted pay their victims for any goods stolen and by contributing time and energy to community service projects.

Today 70 percent of those convicted of crime repeat the offense for which they were convicted. A strong effort will be made to educate and train criminals so that they will not repeat their crime. In some cases this may involve behavior modification training or the use of drugs designed to control aggressive behavior.

Nonviolent criminals may serve their sentences by being confined to their homes or unguarded correction centers. They will be allowed to leave to do public service work or attend counseling sessions. These "inmates" will have small computer chips inserted beneath their skin. Signals from these chips will allow police to constantly monitor the whereabouts of these people.

Those engaged in drug-related crimes will be sent first to drug rehabilitation centers for treatment. If they are unable to overcome their addiction, they will receive chemical substitutes for the drug to which they are addicted. They will then receive smaller and smaller doses until they are "clean." Once rehabilitated, these people will serve sentences for their crimes while learning a skill that will make them useful members of society when they are paroled.

Hardened criminals who cannot be returned to society will work in isolated areas such as deep-sea fish farms, offshore oil rigs, or factories in space. Many of the duties involved in guarding these criminals will be delegated to robots.

These advances in communication technology will have an enormous impact on the society of tomorrow. By reducing the need for transportation, more will work at home. The family unit, whatever its nature, and neighborhoods will be more closely knit. A genuine sense of community and willingness to help others will be reborn.

8

Transportation: From Horse and Buggy to Space Buses

Travel, in the younger sort, is a part of education, in the elder a part of experience.
—Francis Bacon, Of Travel

In today's world of trucks, buses, and cars moving along superhighways and giant passenger and cargo airplanes speeding across continents, the railroad seems almost a relic. Most of you are probably more familiar with air travel than with a long ride by railroad coach. However, in the period between 1865 and 1914, railroads dominated the transportation scene in America.

During the next century superconductor technology will enable us to build railroads that will carry passengers from coast to coast in thirty minutes. And we will see at last a clean, fast, and efficient mass transit system. By 2090 it's likely that space buses will travel to manufacturing centers that orbit the earth. It may even be possible by then to take a vacation cruise, not on the earth's seas, but in orbit well above the earth's sea of air.

American Railroads

Railroads proved their importance during the Civil War. Long forgotten were the early fears of injury to livestock or health hazards as a result of the unheard of speed of fifteen miles per hour. In the post-Civil War period railroads expanded, prospered, and improved. In 1864 George Pullman developed the sleeping car, which received a sad and unexpected boost in recognition when it was used in the funeral train of Abraham Lincoln. The air brake, developed by George Westinghouse in 1869, improved railway safety. In that same year, the work of thousands of Irish and Chinese laborers was finished when Governor Leland Stanford drove a golden spike into the ground at Promontory Point, Utah, marking the completion of the transcontinental railroad. Forty years later, seven railroad lines provided transcontinental service. The decade of the 1870s witnessed further improvements. Railroads established a standard gauge, or width, between rails. This permitted uninterrupted connections and longer runs. Iron rails were replaced with more durable steel tracks. By 1900, the United States had more railroad mileage than all of Europe and Russia combined.

Train travel, even in 1880, could be a physically punishing, mind-numbing, and dangerous experience, however. Most travelers were middle- or working-class people who could not afford the luxury of a private Pullman car. Their second- or third-class tickets provided them with seats that were little more than hard wooden benches. If the seats were upholstered, the material was frequently infested with bugs. Sleep in a day coach was nearly impossible, since the seats had no headrests and noise from fellow passengers and the train itself was unending. Even if a traveler did manage to doze, chances are he or she would be awakened by one of the many boys who peddled newspapers, candy, fruit, and nuts to passengers.

Often dust and heat were annoying as well. Those who could afford them wore linen dusters to protect their clothes when the windows were open. The alternative, a closed window, resulted in an overwhelming odor from the sixty to seventy bodies packed into the boxlike car, combined with tobacco smoke and whiskey fumes. Before the introduction of steam heat, trains were heated by wood- or coal-burning stoves. Experienced travelers tried to sit in the middle of a car. Those near the stove roasted while those at the end of the car opposite the stove froze. Surviving a winter derailment did not ensure escape from a fire caused by an overturned stove. The oil and kerosene lamps used at night were an additional fire hazard.

Dining cars were a welcome luxury when they first appeared in the late 1880s. Prior to this, travelers ate in restaurants during stopovers of ten to thirty minutes. There were more dangerous problems. Boilers, because they were seldom inspected, sometimes exploded. Train robbers, such as Jesse James and Sam Bass, were a constant threat. Frequent water stops and bad weather that caused washouts, flooding, and collapsed bridges were another inconvenience. Small wonder that people were grateful when they arrived at their destinations! Nonetheless, railroads became America's first big business. They changed the country by establishing a model for other giant corporate enterprises that followed.

Railroads reduced the cost of transportation and shortened travel time from weeks or months to hours or days. Railroads were a boon to farmers who could now travel to cities with their crops, providing fresh produce for the urban population. Such a trip was often too long and difficult in a wagon. Railroads also provided swifter, more efficient mail delivery. That made it easier for people to keep in touch with distant relatives. Businesses found it easier than before to expand and become nationwide. Whole new industries developed to meet the demands of the "Iron Horse." Steel, coal, and car manufacturing provided jobs for Americans. Even time was changed by the railroad. Efficient management of rail transportation demanded a standard time for the whole country in place of the local times, determined by the sun, that existed in post-Civil War America. In 1883 railroads established the four continental time zones that we have today. But it was thirty-five years later before Congress made these time zones the law of the land.

Horsepower

Transportation technology improved greatly during the late nineteenth and early twentieth century. Nevertheless, the horse and buggy remained the mainstay of local transportation. In city or country, "Old Dobbin" was counted on to move people and freight. If a family did not own a horse, there were plenty of livery stables where they could rent one, along with a wagon. However, the horse was not without its critics. Horses were major polluters and noise makers. They were slow and possessed limited pulling power.

Manure was the major pollutant. Sanitary experts in the early twentieth century estimated that the average horse dropped twenty pounds of manure a day. Most people accepted this as the price for transportation, but it could be a nuisance. Dried manure, turned to powder, blew into people's faces and homes. On rainy days the manure runoff made streets almost impassable for ladies in long dresses. Today, the horses used for nostalgic tours of the historic district of Charleston, South Carolina, are diapered. This is not a baby's diaper, but a leather bag attached to the harness to catch the droppings. Unfortunately, the cost of diapering the huge number of horses in the 1880s and 1890s made this impossible for our ancestors—if they ever thought of it. The iron shoes of horses pounding on the pavement while pulling a wagon with iron-rimmed wheels created a disturbing racket.

Early Mass-Transit Systems

As cities expanded, horses were pressed into public transport service. The omnibus, an enlarged stagecoach, was the first form of mass transportation in this country. Then, in 1832 in New York City, the success of the railroad inspired a new experiment. To eliminate friction and allow the horse to pull more weight, rails were laid down and the horsecar was born. This remained the major means of urban transportation for the next fifty years.

City life was difficult for horses. They had a short work life and were often mistreated and overworked. Cobblestone pavement was slippery, and horses frequently fell and were injured. The average horse's speed of four to six miles an hour limited the distance a person could travel. The cost of feeding and stabling horses and the ever-present manure combined to make urban travel by horse unsatisfactory. The transportation situation reached a crisis in 1872 when a virus attacked the nation's horses. To keep the cities moving, men were hired to pull the cars and, in some cases, even dogs were put into harness.

Pressured by continued growth in industry and population, cities sought to improve their mass-transportation systems. In 1868 New York City developed the first elevated train system—the El. It was a failure. Homes along the route were abandoned and became slums because of the noise and dirt caused by the trains. Traffic on the streets below was hindered by the iron columns used to support the "streets on stilts." Pedestrians had to dodge falling ash, cinders, and oil. Other cities, most notably Boston and Chicago, built elevated trains, too, but theirs came later and were much cleaner because the trains were powered by electricity, not coal.

For a fleeting moment in history, the transportation problems of the cities appeared to be solved when Andrew S. Hallidie invented the cable car. Hallidie was a prosperous businessman by 1869. His early success was in making wire rope for California mining operations and supplying cables for suspension bridges. One rainy morning in San Francisco, he watched a horsecar struggle to pull a load of freight up a steep hill. The horse slipped, fell, and was dragged down the hill and had to be destroyed. The unfortunate incident gave Hallidie an idea.

His idea was simple. He would place a continuously running three-inch cable between railroad tracks in an underground trough about two feet deep and eighteen inches wide. A steam engine at the end of the line would power the cable. A system of pulleys in the trough would direct the cable around corners. The passenger car would be attached to the cable by a viselike "grip" that the operator could open and close with a lever. The speed of the cable was controlled at the power house; it determined the speed of the car connected to it. To stop the car, the operator simply loosened the "grip." That allowed the cable to slide through the clamp. The operator then applied the brakes to the wheels. At the end of the line, the car dropped the cable completely and rotated on a turntable for the return trip.

To prevent any loss of public faith and to avoid embarrassment, the test run of the first cable car was scheduled at three o'clock in the morning on August 1, 1873. One look up the steep Clay Street hill convinced the ex-locomotive engineer, who was to be the first gripman, or operator, that the danger involved was not worth the salary he was to be paid. He resigned on the spot, and Hallidie himself made the first round trip in a cable car at a speed of four miles per hour. The test run was a success and the cable car began to make regular runs in September 1873.

The advantages of the system were obvious. It was quiet and clean, it maintained a steady rate of speed, which had increased to ten miles per hour by 1890, and it could carry large loads. However, the construction of cable systems was expensive. That restricted its use to large cities where the volume of passengers made it profitable. The cable had to be replaced yearly, and gripmen had to be specially trained. The moving cable was an open invitation to children, who tied their wagons and sleds to it. Sometimes the cable would shred so that the car could not be stopped. As late as 1971, an accident of this kind in San Francisco cost the city $100,000 in damages. In 1967 two people were killed and thirty injured in a similar mishap.

Today, tourists have to travel to San Francisco to ride the only remaining cable car system, but in the 1880s, cities from New York to Seattle and as far away as Europe and New Zealand developed cable lines. The popularity of the cable car peaked in the early 1890s when a new, less expensive, and faster mass transit system appeared. It was the trolley!

Transport by Trolley

From 1890 until the 1920s, when it was gradually displaced by the automobile, the electric trolley was the most heavily used form of mass transportation in the country. The trolley became what the automobile is to the modern family. For five cents it carried Father to work, the children to school, and the entire family downtown for shopping on Saturday and to church on Sunday. There were even special funeral cars for a person's last ride.

The idea of electric propulsion was not new. Charles De Poele ran an experimental line in Toronto, Canada, in 1885 and in Montgomery, Alabama, in 1886. These small lines were plagued by mechanical difficulties. But De Poele was finally successful in devising an electric power source for trolley cars that was driven by steam. The trolley pole that extended from the car was a pivoting rod with a rotating contact wheel on one end. This was held against the underside of the overhead electric power line by means of spring tension.

But it was Frank J. Sprague, a U.S. Naval Academy graduate and former associate of Thomas Edison, who developed the first reliable, durable, and profitable electric trolley transport system. In 1887 Sprague accepted a contract to build a power plant, install twelve miles of track with overhead wires, and build and run forty cars for the city of Richmond, Virginia. Sprague overcame numerous obstacles, including poor construction contractors and a bout with typhoid fever, to complete the line. He lost $75,000 in the process but gained a reputation that led the large Boston West End Railway to request his help in bringing the electric trolley to Boston.

Soon trolleys were everywhere. Brooklyn, New York, had so many lines that Brooklynites were nicknamed "Trolley Dodgers." The nickname was so closely associated with the people of the borough that they called their baseball team the Dodgers. Ironically, after the trolleys ceased running in Brooklyn, the Dodgers moved to Los Angeles. Trolley lines between cities began to compete with steam trains for freight and passengers. By the turn of the century, electrically powered transportation was one of America's biggest businesses.

The open car, inherited from the horsecar era, was the most popular vehicle on the line. In the days before air conditioning, a ride on one of these "breezer" cars was an ideal escape from the oppressive summer heat. But open cars could be operated only in the summer, which necessitated another set of cars for winter. Also, the original design of long benches and no center aisle made it

Transportation 117

Without air-conditioning the "breezer car" of America's trolley system was the best way to cool off on a hot summer day.

difficult to collect fares. Companies eventually created convertible cars with windows that could be removed in the summer to allow a free flow of air, and a center aisle to be sure fares were collected.

In an effort to increase riders during nonpeak hours, companies encouraged the establishment of on-line amusement parks to attract children. Similarly, trolley companies published tour guides extolling the virtues of fresh air and scenery beyond the city. Trolleys could be chartered for parties, group travel, or company picnics.

By today's standards, the trolley was slow, but it provided economical, reliable, and convenient travel for our ancestors. It expanded people's horizons and allowed them to travel beyond the inner city. Even longer trolley lines with frequent stops led to the development of suburbs. Equally important, the trolley allowed travel for travel's sake, something only the wealthy had done regularly before the 1890s.

The automobile made its first appearance in this country in 1894 and gradually began to cut into the trolley business. By 1920—except for a brief revival during World War II, when tire and gas rationing increased its popularity—the trolley industry was dying. In fact, automobile and tire companies tried to ensure the popularity of the automobile by buying trolley companies, junking their equipment, and closing the lines. The last trolleys were built in the United States in 1951. Of the nine cities that operate trolley lines today, only New Orleans has a traditional trolley line. Most systems are rapid transit systems that use streamlined, lightweight cars. Trolley buffs, environmentalists, and others were heartened, however, by the recent announcement that Los Angeles, a stronghold of automobile commuters, will construct a new trolley system to relieve traffic congestion.

From Trolleys to Cars

During the twentieth century in America, the automobile gradually replaced the trolley in cities and the horse in rural areas. By using parts (gears, rods, rings, and so forth) that were all the same and by introducing the assembly line, Henry Ford mass-produced a relatively inexpensive car, the Model T. Henry Ford's methods revolutionized the nation's transportation and its society as well. Car owners were free to travel wherever they wished whenever they wished. Commuting by car from a rural home to an urban job became common. Horses became farm animals, not a means of transportation. Even on farms, most horses were replaced by trucks and tractors after World War II.

Today the automobile is our primary means of transportation. Even in metropolitan areas where mass transit systems are available, many people drive to work. The results of America's love of the automobile are traffic jams, polluted air, and the demise of railroads.

Tomorrow's Transportation and Energy

The cars of tomorrow will depend to a large extent on the energy of the future. Early in the twenty-first century it is likely that scientists and engineers will learn how to control the fusion of hydrogen and helium isotopes. When hydrogen atoms fuse (unite) to form helium, huge amounts of energy are released.

Today we lack the ability to control this process that occurs naturally in stars and is the origin of the vast quantities of energy that they emit. It was the uncontrolled fusion of hydrogen that provided the energy released in the explosion of hydrogen bombs that were developed and tested after World War II. Considerable progress has been made in controlling fusion. At the moment, however, more energy is required to initiate the fusion process than is released by the small quantities of hydrogen that unite to form helium.

Photovoltaic cells, which can change light to electricity, will remain the primary means of generating electrical energy in space. But by 2090, controlled fusion may replace coal, oil, and nuclear fission as the main source of electrical power on earth. Some electricity will still be generated by hydroelectric, OTEC, geothermal, waste, windmills, and solar power plants. However, the use of fossil fuels to produce electricity will have declined along with their availability. Though fusion power may eventually replace wind- and sun-powered plants, electricity generated from waste will be retained as an efficient method for dealing with trash and garbage. As a result, the world's air and water will be cleaner. Our descendants will live in a more healthful environment than we.

The Cars of Tomorrow

A century from now aerodynamically styled automobiles equipped with computerized mapping systems will be common. An early version of these cars can be seen in the World of Motion exhibit in EPCOT Center at Walt Disney World Resort near Orlando, Florida. Such cars will

Transportation

be made of plastics and composites reinforced with glass or carbon fibers. Computer-controlled ceramic engines and transmissions will provide transportation in an efficient manner. Joined by strong gluelike adhesives, not welds, the materials used to make these cars will not corrode. Their plastic bodies will have elastic qualities that will cause them to spring back to their original shape when dented. Consequently, the cars of tomorrow, in keeping with the twenty-first century commitment to conserving our natural resources, will last for decades.

The rapid-transit system of the future will feature small electrically powered cars. Programmed by a ticket, the car will proceed automatically through the system to the passengers' destination without stopping enroute. Illus.: Taxi 2000 Corp.

Technological advances will make cars safer and easier to drive. Holograms showing the car's speed will be visible above the hood. A radar avoidance system will automatically brake the car if it gets too close to a vehicle ahead of it. As an additional safety measure, an alcohol-detecting device will prevent the car from starting if the driver has been drinking.

By 2090 it is likely that hydrogen fusion power plants will have reduced the cost of electrical energy significantly. As a result, electric engines in automobiles and trucks will replace today's internal combustion motors, which burn expensive fuels such as gasoline, kerosene, and alcohol.

Trucks, like cars, will be more streamlined. They will have skirts covering the wheels and folding flanges between tractor and trailer to further reduce air resistance. In addition to a dashboard map, trucks will have a computer to direct the driver along the most efficient route, based on the location of all the deliveries that are to be made.

Return of the Railroad

The railroads of the nineteenth and twentieth centuries will never return. Nevertheless, materials that are superconductors at room temperature will bring dramatic changes in rail travel. Superconductors, which are expected to be in use in the near future, are materials that offer no resistance to the flow of electric charge. They will make it possible for us to build very strong electromagnets. Electromagnets on the railroad cars will be repelled by electromagnets on the rails. This will make it

In the rapid-transit car the passengers will ride in privacy. Illus.: Taxi 2000 Corp.

possible to produce magnetically levitated trains that will glide frictionlessly along guide rails. Additional superconducting electromagnets will be used to push and pull the train along its path at speeds as high as 300 miles per hour.

Such high-speed, smooth-riding trains may well connect the cities of the future. In fact, early in the twenty-second century similar trains, powered by fusion-generated plasma jets, may move across and between continents inside large vacuum tubes. The plasma, which consists of positive gaseous ions and the electrons that have been stripped from them, will be generated by heat from fusion engines. It will then be directed into a jet by strong magnets produced by large electric currents in superconducting coils. Air will be evacuated from large tubes, making resistance to motion virtually zero. These trains may carry you across the country, from New York to Los Angeles, in thirty minutes. Similar tubes beneath the English Channel and the Bering Strait will allow peo-

THE FUTURE AND THE PAST

ple to commute from England to France or from North America to Asia.

A Less Massive Mass Transit System

In large cities mass transit systems may still use the subway tunnels of today, but the trains will be magnetically levitated cars that will move swiftly and quietly from place to place. In smaller cities, buses and subways will give way to small two-, three-, or four-passenger cars on elevated rails. These electrically powered cars will have air-filled tires that roll along plastic guide rails, providing a smooth, quiet ride at speeds varying from fifteen to sixty miles per hour depending on the amount of traffic. Since most automobiles will be barred from cities, these

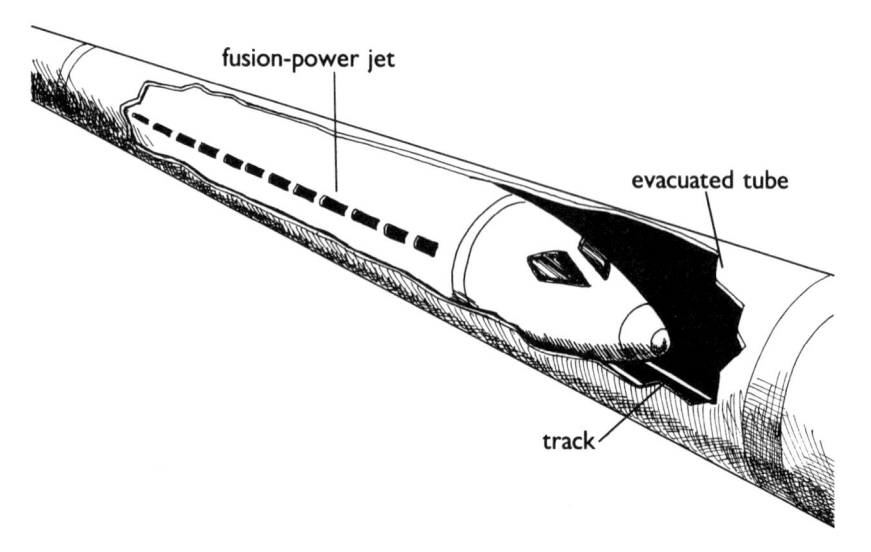

"The Tube" will have a different meaning when these plasma jet-powered trains cross the country in less than a half hour in the twenty-second century.

Transportation 125

small rapid transit cars will be the only means of transportation, other than bicycles and walking, in many cities.

At terminals, where these small cars will arrive in rapid succession, you will use your credit card to enter the station. You'll then punch your destination and the number of passengers into a computer that will direct you to the correct track and car number for boarding. Once you enter the car and close the door, it will automatically carry you to your destination along the fastest possible route.

The New "El" will be quiet and nonpolluting. It will "chauffeur" your descendants throughout the city quickly and efficiently. Illus.: Taxi 2000 Corp.

THE FUTURE AND THE PAST

Air and Space Travel of the Future

Like cars, airplanes of the future will be made of lighter, stronger materials that generate less drag force than do the metals used today. Carbon fibers embedded in epoxy plastics will probably replace the aluminum used in today's planes. More efficient prop-fan engines with eight blades, each resembling a Turkish sword (scimitar), may replace today's jet engines. Giant 600-passenger planes

This is a twenty-second- or twenty-third-century space colony. Each of the twin cylinders is 19 miles long and 4 miles in diameter. Here more than 200,000 people may one day reside. The rings of "tea cups" are agricultural stations. A manufacturing center extends forward from each colony. The winglike flaps are mirrors used to reflect sunlight into the colonies. Photo: NASA

Transportation

will ferry people across oceans and continents at velocities two to three times the speed of sound. For those who need to travel even faster, sleek planes powered by combustion ramjet engines will rise rapidly to the altitudes of satellites before descending to points halfway around the world. Those who are willing to pay the price will be able to fly to any major city in the world in two hours.

Giant helium-filled lighter-than-air ships will carry

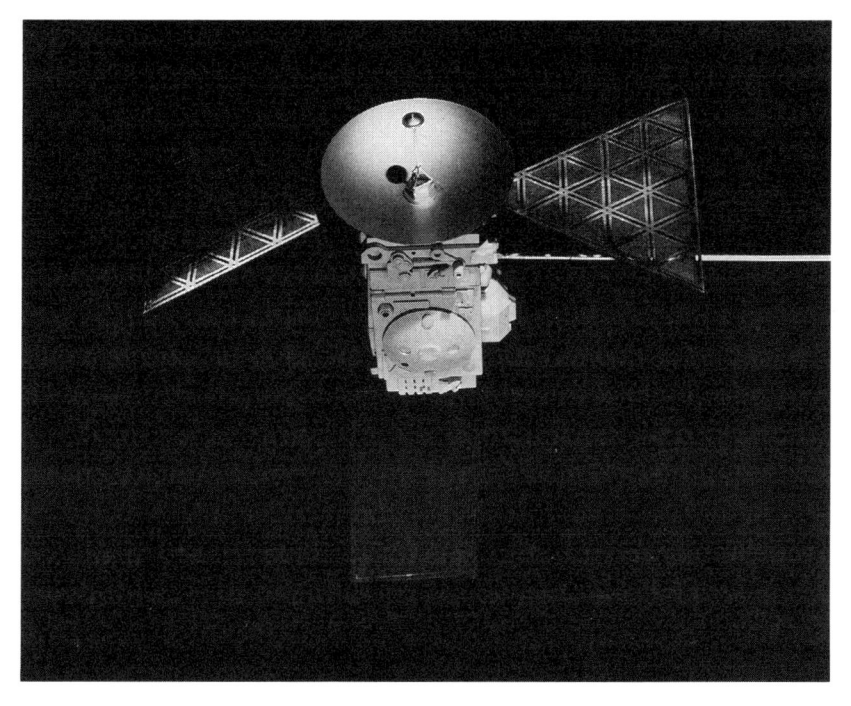

A model of a manufacturing facility where lunar rocks will be converted into aluminum, glass, and other materials. The "wings" are solar panels that convert sunlight into electricity.
Photo: NASA

cargo and passengers slowly but efficiently across continents. Just as many people today spend their vacations on ocean cruises, so our ancestors will enjoy elevated views of relatively uninhabited jungles and prairies and the wildlife of these areas.

The jet-powered backpacks that enable astronauts to maneuver in space will, in the future, allow police, fire fighters, and reporters to move over crowds, traffic jams, and other barriers.

About a century from now, our descendants may travel beyond the moon to other planets, such as Mars, and to the moons of Jupiter on spaceships powered by hot plasma jets. Two or three centuries from now, once bases are established on Mars and the moons of Jupiter, giant spaceships powered by fusion engines may travel to the nearest stars. The stars chosen will be those that appear to have planets in orbit about them. Until such trips are made, we will probably not know whether other forms of intelligent life exist in our galaxy.

9

Food and Agriculture: From Family Farm to Community Greenhouse

Tell me what you eat and I will tell you what you are!
—Anthelme Brillat-Savarin, Physiologie du goât

As the nineteenth century drew to a close, farming was still America's major occupation. It involved 43 percent of the population as opposed to about 3 percent today. You might guess that farmers of that era were prosperous and enjoyed more leisure time than their fathers. Urban growth had created a tremendous demand for food. Harvesting machines, first drawn by horses and later powered by steam, eased the burden of farmwork. Scientific improvements, such as "Russian" wheat that could withstand climatic extremes, reduced the need for water. Improved railroads allowed for better marketing of goods and enabled farmers to cultivate lands that were formerly inaccessible. In fact, more new land was cultivated between 1870 and 1900 than had been farmed in all the nation's previous years combined.

Nonetheless, farmers often suffered from these improvements, and the period was a time of great agricultural discontent.

By the end of the twenty-first century intensive farming—made possible by technology, plant breeding, and genetic engineering—will actually reduce the amount of land used to grow food. Fewer farmers will produce more food on less land. An increase in fish farming will make greater use of the sea and freshwater ponds. The uncultivated land will become forests again, providing shelter for an increasing number of wild animals.

Westward Ho!

Farming, like population, shifted westward to the Great Plains as the nineteenth century drew to a close. But the rural life there was very difficult. Many of the things considered necessities in the East were unavailable on the plains. For example, because there were few trees, there was no wood for fuel or to build homes or fences. Farmers dug their homes out of the sides of hills. These "dugouts" and "soddies," houses made from "bricks" of sod cut from the prairie, became home for farm families. They were impossible to keep clean. Bugs were a constant problem for the diligent housewife. The space was cold and damp when it rained. Dried manure—"buffalo chips"—was used for fuel. A means of fencing farmland became available in 1874 when Joseph Glidden invented barbed wire. The wire fences allowed ranching and farming in the same areas by keeping cattle on the range and away from crops.

It was a lonely and boring life, especially for farm women. Their husbands could at least change the nature of their work as chores and seasons varied, and they made trips to town to buy supplies or sell crops. But a woman's work in the home seldom varied, though often she would work beside her husband in the fields. The distance between farms required travel and time women could ill afford. Consequently, contact with neighbors was infrequent. Unaided and unsupported by relatives or friends, the western farm wife faced a life-style vastly different from what she had known in the East. The pressures on her to solve domestic crises, aid in her husband's work, run a good home, and deal with family illnesses and injuries were tremendous.

Climate presented yet another obstacle for the farmer. Scorched, parched summers and freezing temperatures with drifting snows in winter were uncontrollable and unpredictable. The unusually wet weather of the 1870s and early 1880s convinced many emigrants that they could eventually prosper on the plains, and this hope lulled settlers into a false sense of security. When the normal dry summer weather pattern returned, the droughts were devastating. One story, told many times, was about the farmer who was hit by a drop of rain and could be revived only after being doused with several buckets of dry dirt. But even good weather did not relieve the farmer's plight. Plagues of insects, largely grasshoppers, ravaged farmland. As one farmer stated: "The hoppers only left the mortgage."

Technology held great promise for these farmers, but it ultimately failed them. To compete with established

This Nebraska farm family posed for this photo on top of their horse-pulled reaper at wheat harvest time. Photo: UPI/Bettmann Newsphotos

eastern farms where yields were larger, prairie farmers had to buy expensive machinery. This meant obtaining a loan from a local bank, using land or livestock as collateral. Increased production caused prices to drop. To compensate for lower prices, the farmer tried to produce larger crops. This led to overproduction, drained the land of its fertility, and caused prices to decline further. When a farmer exhausted his credit and failed to meet mortgage payments, the bank foreclosed, took his land, and set the farmer adrift.

To combat this economic plight, farmers began to specialize in a cash crop that would consistently provide a good income. Certain regions of the country became associated with a specific crop. For example, Minnesota and New England became dairy centers. The corn belt was in Iowa and the Midwest. Wheat was the crop of the plains. Unfortunately, this system caused farmers to lose some of their independence. They began to depend on others for modern goods and services, even for food. Success depended on new equipment, bigger farms, and increased specialization. The American ideal of the independent, self-sufficient farmer was largely history by the end of the nineteenth century. Farming had become big business.

Big Eating: An American Custom

The demand for agricultural products was unceasing. Eating was something Americans did with gusto, and having enough to eat was important to them. Americans ate more and better than the people of any other nation. This is not to say there were no hungry Americans. The poor often lived on tea and bread or bought the cheapest food possible. Most cities had secondhand food stores where markets dumped damaged products and stale baked goods. Butchers sent their scraps to these stores to be sold to the poor. Yet the immigrants who ate this food wrote home to tell of the abundance of food in America and how good it was.

Beef and pork, in its many forms—chops or bacon, for example—were staples of the American diet. Potatoes, bread, and pastries were also found on most American tables. Meals were larger than they are today and centered around protein and starches.

Steak and coffee were the most frequent breakfast foods, although pork chops, codfish, and eggs were sometimes substituted. The steaks were thin-cut, tossed in flour, and fried. The meat was served with a creamy gravy made of the pan drippings combined with flour and milk. Fruit was also an important part of the day's first meal. Oranges were popular, but not as juice. People ate oranges the way we eat grapefruit today. For those who found fresh fruit too costly, stewed prunes served as an alternative. Prunes had the added attraction of offering relief from the national curse—constipation caused by overeating.

TABLE 1. Food Prices in 1890

Food Item (1 pound of)	Cost (in cents)
Bacon	12.5
Bread	14.5
Butter	25.5
Eggs (1 dozen)	20.8
Milk (½ gallon delivered)	13.6
Potatoes	16.0
Round steak	14.5

Source: U.S. Bureau of the Census, 1890.

A hundred years ago, which was more expensive, steak or bread?

Breakfast on board trains was amazing. Ham and eggs, fried oysters, fried chicken, sausage, fried potatoes, hot biscuits, corn bread, pancakes, and coffee seemed standard. It was clear that Americans loved their food, especially if it was fried.

Not everyone viewed a hearty breakfast as healthy, and a minor revolution in American eating was begun by Dr. John H. Kellogg of Battle Creek, Michigan, and his competitors. Kellogg was the doctor in charge of the Battle Creek Sanitarium, a health hospital for the wealthy. Through his research on diet, Kellogg developed a precooked flake he thought could be used as a snack. He called it Granola. His patients, however, began eating it for breakfast with milk and sweeteners. At about the same time, in 1893, Henry D. Perky of Denver invented a process for making what he called Shredded Wheat. In 1898, Charles W. Post, a former patient of Kellogg's, developed his own breakfast food, Grape Nuts. The name was derived from the product's nutty taste and the fact that it contained maltose, which Post called grape sugar. The success of Grape Nuts led Post to patent Post Toasties, an imitation of Kellogg's flakes, and Postum, a coffee substitute made of bran, wheat, and molasses. Americans were impressed by the convenience of these new cold breakfast cereals and began to eat them regularly.

Lunch, which was commonly called dinner in 1890, was even more substantial than breakfast. Two meats, gravy, vegetables, cheese, and pickles made up the main course. Pudding or pie followed, and usually some fruit to hold hunger off until dinner. Dinner—usually called supper in 1890—was very similar, except that potatoes were added to the menu.

Gathering for a picnic brought a welcome break in the daily routine. Photo: Culver Pictures, Inc.

This description of the 1890 American diet does not reveal the ugliness that was a part of food at the time. Most Americans of the period were born on farms or in the country. They recalled raising, processing, and storing what they ate. What they could not raise for themselves, they got from neighbors or through the local store owner. They had some sense of control over what they ate because they had grown it themselves or bought it from neighbors or a local store. When the country began to urbanize, this changed. A city resident could not be sure who handled his food, where it came from, or whether canned foods were safe or spoiled. Knowing this, food

Food and Agriculture

merchants took advantage of consumers. To meet the growing food demands of urbanites, grocers and vendors attempted to stretch their food supplies by adulteration—adding extra inert ingredients.

Dairy products had materials added to them. Water, chalk, and plaster of paris were used to "stretch" milk. Some distilleries kept cattle and fed them the mash that was left over from the whiskey-making process. "Swill milk," produced from cows who ate this mash, was said to make children slightly drunk. Slaughterhouses boiled down meat they could not sell, added some fat, and sold it as butter. Canned peas were treated with green salts of copper to give them that garden-fresh look.

The Embalmed Beef Scandal occurred during the Spanish-American War of 1898 when American troops received old, tainted beef doctored to look and smell fresh. Though the scandal upset the public, it was not until the 1906 publication of *The Jungle,* by Upton Sinclair, which documented the horrors of the stockyard, that Americans took action to ensure the purity of their food and medicine through legislation designed to protect consumers.

Water—A Crucial Factor in the Farms of the Future

Water levels in the aquifers (underground reservoirs of water) that supply water for many farms today are dropping at an alarming rate. Rivers, another source of water, cannot meet the nation's needs, either. For example, the Colorado River, which is used to irrigate farms in a number of western states and Mexico, is reduced to a trickle

THE FUTURE AND THE PAST 138

by the time it reaches the sea. Yet the demand for water continues to increase.

Over the next century a number of approaches will be used to meet the crisis of an ever-shrinking water supply. This problem is compounded by a growing migration of people to the dry Southwest. There are plans to pump water from the Great Lakes and western Canada to supplement the Colorado River and the giant Ogallala Aquifer, which extends from South Dakota to Texas. But such a solution would cost billions of dollars. The huge dams that would be needed to trap Canadian water would flood a vast area of land with unforeseen ecological effects.

Another scheme involves towing giant icebergs from the Antarctic to the coast of southern California. Others include spreading carbon black over the surface of Alaskan glaciers to increase their melting rate and distilling or freezing seawater to separate the water from the dissolved salts.

It is more likely that less expensive methods will be used during the next hundred years to meet the nation's water crisis. Improved methods of treating and recycling waste water will allow much of the water that we now dump into septic systems and sewers to be reused. However, water for domestic use is but a small fraction of the water used to irrigate crops on western farms. More than three-fourths of our water is used for agriculture. Of the water taken from western rivers, 85 percent flows onto irrigated farmland. More than half of that water is lost through evaporation.

We can learn much from Israel about making the best use of a limited water supply. There, deserts have been

Food and Agriculture

turned into green fields despite an annual natural rainfall of only twenty-five inches. By spreading silver iodide crystals on clouds, Israelis have been able to induce rain, thereby increasing their rainfall by 15 percent. A system of drip irrigation in which buried pipes deliver water to plant roots has been developed. This method eliminates the evaporation losses that are so large in ditch and sprinkler systems. A national policy of water development and taxation encourages recycling and conservation while discouraging the waste of this precious resource. Hydrological engineering reduces water losses and makes maximum use of available moisture. By careful breeding of

The drip irrigation tubing that runs along the ground carries water to the roots of each of these plants growing in dry soil.
© The Walt Disney Company

plants, the Israelis have produced miniature fruit trees and vegetables that require relatively little water. These methods are only a few of the ways in which Israel has used science and technology to overcome a severe shortage of water.

The Intensive Farming of the Future

It is likely that farming a century from now will be more intensive—that is, the space used to grow food, particularly fruits and vegetables, will be reduced. This change in farming technique will come about for many reasons. One reason is that the shortage of water will become increasingly acute. A second is that the emergence of a strong sense of community will lead to neighborhood farms similar to those found at the New Alchemy Institute in Falmouth, Massachusetts. A third reason is that genetic engineers will develop plants that require less water, produce more fruit, and are disease-resistant. Fourth, a more healthful diet will increase our consumption of foods that require relatively little space for growth such as vegetables, fish, and poultry. At the same time, foods that require large growing areas—such as beef, pork, and lamb—will be less popular.

A pound of beans or kelp has as much protein as two pounds of steak, but the steak's flavor makes it a more popular food. In the future, genetic engineers will probably develop plants that contain the beneficial proteins and flavor of meat without the harmful fats that are believed to be related to heart disease. When they do, eating foods that are good for us will not seem so onerous.

Of course, insects and worms are a rich source of protein, too. Who knows? By 2090 such protein sources may be more widely accepted as food than they are today. After all, people used to think that tomatoes were poisonous.

As a result of dietary changes, there will be less demand for grain to fatten animals and grasses for grazing, both of which require abundant acreage.

Prosumer Community Farms

In his book, *The Third Wave,* Alvin Toffler writes about "prosumers," people who both produce and consume. Today we tend to divide the population into farmers, those who produce food, and consumers, the other 97 percent of the population, who buy the food and consume it. In the future, the division between producer and consumer will probably be less sharp. More communities will establish neighborhood gardens and greenhouses where fresh vegetables and fish will be grown year-round. In rural communities an abundance of produce, including wheat, will be grown for sale to urban areas.

It will remain more expensive to grow food in greenhouses and local gardens than in large fields. However, producing food locally eliminates transportation costs, which will increase as fuel becomes more costly. Making food available locally also will reduce waste and ensure fresh food. It will even reduce the need for additives currently used to preserve food.

These different plants grow side by side. The stems of the larger plants are supported, and their roots exposed to the air.
© The Walt Disney Company

Food and Agriculture

In areas where rainfall is minimal, water will be supplied to the plants by means of drip irrigation. To reduce water needs and the space devoted to agriculture, intercropping will become more common. For example, squash vines will grow on frames and will provide shade for shade-tolerant spinach, which will grow beneath the vines. Cornstalks will serve as supports for the vines of bean plants. (This will be especially good for those farmers who want to grow succotash.)

In some greenhouses, plants will be started in soil and then transferred to Styrofoam-like supports. Their exposed roots will rest in a fine mist generated from troughs of nutrient fluid. In these troughs fish will grow in abundance. These greenhouses will supply both fresh vegetables and fish.

During winter months in cold climates, greenhouses will be insulated at night or on stormy days by means of foam beads. The beads will be blown into and evacuated from a space surrounding the structures. Artificial lighting will extend the hours of daylight for those plants that require long days to grow properly.

Some fishless greenhouses will grow plants by means of hydroponics—that is, the roots will rest in nutrient solutions, not in soil. Such a system will allow each type of plant to receive exactly the right amount of the particular nutrients that are unique to it. Near these greenhouses one will likely find aquaculture centers where tons of fish will be grown in indoor ponds.

If you visit the Land exhibit in EPCOT Center at Walt Disney World Resort near Orlando, Florida, you can see many of these future farming methods for yourself.

Open Land and Water

Not all the food in the future will be grown in community gardens, greenhouses, and aquaria. There will still be some large farms. But a century from now, genetic engineers and breeders will have produced grasses and grains that require less water to grow, chickens that produce more eggs, and animals that grow faster and leaner (to reduce the fat in beef, pork, and lamb). With less land required to grow crops and graze sheep and cattle, more land will be declared open and allowed to return to its natural state where wild plants and animals will flourish.

Because fish are a more efficient source of protein than beef, pork, sheep, and chickens, fish farms will be more common than they are today. Some will be in the ocean, as we mentioned in Chapter 3. Certain fish farms may specialize in Caribbean king crabs where, some futurists predict, it may be possible to produce 900 million tons of crabs a year—more than the world's present annual production of meat.

Some floating sea farms associated with OTEC electric power centers will grow salt-tolerant plants whose roots will dangle in seawater. Both the plants and the fish that swim in the fish farms beneath them will be nourished by nutrients pumped up from the cold ocean depths to cool the fluid used in generating electricity at these floating power plants.

Not all fish farmers will live in or on the sea, however. Some will reside on country farms similar to those of today. There they may alternate a crop of soybeans with a crop of catfish, which will eat soybean stubble. Other

Food and Agriculture

fish farmers will reside along rivers that empty into the sea. They will release young salmon into these rivers, and the salmon will return to their birthplace two years later to spawn. The larger adult salmon will be sold as food, while the young fish that hatch will be nurtured until they are large enough to be released into the river.

On large fruit and truck farms the picking and harvesting will be done by robots. Fruit trees will be trimmed into cubic shapes to make spraying with insecticides easier. A robot truck will place a cube-shaped plastic cover over the tree so that no insecticide will reach the ground and enter the aquifer. Of course, spraying fruit trees and other crops may become unnecessary if genetic engineers are able to stay ahead in the seemingly never-ending race to produce disease- and insect-resistant trees and plants.

10

Health and Medicine: From Patent Medicines to Self-Care and Computerized Diagnoses

Trust no future howe'er pleasant!
—Lorrey, A Song of Life

For most nineteenth-century Americans, the doctor was not the immediate answer to an illness. Most called a neighbor, consulted a book of home cures, or went to the local druggist before seeking a doctor's advice. Medicine, in 1890, was just beginning to change from a trade to the respected profession it became in the twentieth century.

Today common childhood diseases such as measles, mumps, chicken pox, and whooping cough have been virtually eliminated. As a result, the average life span of Americans has increased dramatically.

By 2090 the growing emphasis on physical fitness together with advances in self-care will make us a nation of healthier, longer-lived people. For those with serious disorders, advances in medical technology will provide artificial organs and better methods of obtaining and preserving living organs for transplants. At the same time, medical research will lead to a variety of unforeseen breakthroughs that will not only save lives but will also improve the quality of life for all who are sick, injured, or disabled.

Medicine: From Trade to Profession

Prior to 1873, just about anyone could become a doctor. Few doctors received a formal education. Most learned the trade and earned the right to practice by serving an apprenticeship. A few who could afford it went to Europe for a formal medical education. Even after 1884, when medical school was extended to three years, American medical schools were inadequate. When Dr. Charles Eliot of Harvard called for written exams, he was reminded by the dean of the school that most medical students could not write well enough to pass them. Prior to the establishment of a model American medical school at Johns Hopkins University in 1893, the only admission requirements for medical school were a grammar school education and the ability to pay the tuition.

By the 1860s, Joseph Lister's germ theory had become well known, and it was generally accepted by the 1880s. Nonetheless, doctors seemed to have an aversion to cleanliness. Major operations were uncommon and used only as a last resort because the accompanying blood loss, shock, and infection were generally beyond the doctor's control. When they did perform surgery, doctors wore street clothes, often used the same dressings and sponges over and over, and stuck their needles in their lapels for safekeeping. Antiseptic surgery did not arrive in the United States until the 1890s.

This is not to say doctors were ineffective. Many of their treatments are common today. Opium was used to control pain, digitalis for heart pain, and aspirin for common aches and pains and fever.

Beginning in the 1880s, there was a movement toward specialization in fields like pediatrics, dermatology, obstetrics, and neurology. By 1884, specialization dominated urban practices while the general practitioner held sway in the countryside.

Although hospitals were still mainly an urban institution, there was a growing acceptance of them as a place for medical care. Prior to 1870, the hospital was seen as a place to die, an unsanitary pesthole, or a place where only the very poor went for treatment. Respectable people avoided hospitals. Your forebears probably received their medical care at home. "Kitchen operations" were common in the practice of most physicians.

By the 1890s, with improved sanitation and the increasing availability of diagnostic testing, hospitals were more generally accepted. The germ theory convinced the public that the very ill should be in sanitary surroundings where others could not be infected. Renewed confidence in the hospital was indicated by the number of women who were admitted for childbirth. Further, families saw the hospital as a way to relieve themselves of the burden of caring for relatives with long-term sicknesses.

The patent medicine industry thrived on those who lacked faith in the medical establishment. Promoted as natural medicines derived from old folk remedies or Native American cures, these products contributed to the era's reputation for quackery. No ailment was without a cure if you believed the advertisements. They promised a cure for everything from cancer to baldness to bad breath. Even animals could be cured if the concoctions were used correctly. Kickapoo Indian Medicine, Hostetler's Stomach Bitters, Lydia Pinkham's Vegetable Compound, and other medicines could be found in American homes well into the twentieth century.

There were two major problems with patent medicines. First, the peddlers were frauds, and they were dangerous, because they offered cures for everything—even incurable diseases such as cancer. Medical neglect of curable diseases by those who used patent medicines led to many unnecessary deaths. Second, the medicines were laced with alcohol and other harmful and addictive drugs. For example, Dr. King's New Discovery for Consumption contained chloroform and opium. It did calm the patient and silence tubercular coughs, but it had no effect on the germ that caused the disease. Similarly, Lydia Pinkham's Vegetable Compound was 18 percent alcohol, Dr. Ayer's Sarsaparilla was 26 percent alcohol, and Hostetler's Bitters contained a whopping 44 percent alcohol. As temperance forces grew, many gained comfort in knowing they could escape the censure of those opposed to alcoholic drinks simply by going to the drugstore for "medicine."

The drug problem is not new. In the 1890s there were no regulations on drugs. Only the cost controlled the drugs a sick person might take. When a prescription ran out, it was simply refilled. Your great-great grandparents dosed themselves with mercury, arsenic, cocaine, and morphine.

Societal changes contributed to a demand for better health care in the United States. A child-centered society that took parental responsibility seriously and sought better health care and survival rates for their offspring played a key role in forcing improvements on the medical profession.

The decade of the 1880s saw an amazing array of medical discoveries that led to the practice of preventive medicine. Inspired by Louis Pasteur's work in 1881 and Theobald Smith's in 1886, immunization through vaccination became a standard treatment. Vaccination involves injections of vaccine developed from the organism that causes the disease and made harmless in a laboratory. In 1980, for example, the World Health Organization declared that the threat of smallpox was over as a result of worldwide vaccination. In 1886, under Smith's guidance, George Washington University established the first bacteriology department in America. German bacteriologist Robert Koch isolated the tuberculosis germ in 1882 and the cholera germ in 1883. The promise of controlling tuberculosis, the nation's greatest killer, and cholera, the most feared epidemic, led to demands for sanitation. Cities and states organized permanent boards of health to improve sanitary conditions. Sanitation in food packaging also improved. By 1880, machines could make tin cans that allowed a more varied diet and ensured a tighter seal than the soldered handmade version.

Doctors of the age got a disturbing preview of the challenges their twentieth-century colleagues would face. Our ancestors suffered primarily from infectious diseases caused by bacteria or viruses transmitted from person to person. Cholera, measles, and tuberculosis were a few of the diseases that regularly assaulted people. One by one these were conquered through scientific discoveries and improved treatment. As the industrial age progressed and life expectancy increased, however, other diseases became increasingly common.

Cancer, cardiac problems, nerve disorders, and other degenerative diseases wore the body down over extended periods of time. There seemed to be no simple causes or cures for these ailments. Heredity, diet, and exposure to hazards in the workplace all contributed to these illnesses. We continue today to search, with increasing hope, for cures for these disorders.

The average life expectancy in the 1890s was just over forty years, but a child who survived infancy could hope to live almost as long as we do today. People began to expect health standards to improve even further, and in the twentieth century, they sought not only protection from death, but relief from minor aches and pains as well. The great advances in medicine during this period were the longer life expectancy that resulted from the development of vaccines, and better education for doctors and nurses.

Today's Life-Style

We tend to think that lives could be saved and the average life span extended by improvements in medicine, but, in fact, 50 percent of the deaths in this country can be attributed to unhealthful behavior and life-style, 20 percent to environmental causes, 10 percent to biological factors, and only 20 percent to inadequate health care. In other words, 80 percent of deaths would not be delayed by improved medical technology.

The major cause of death is heart disease, followed by stroke, cancer, accidents, respiratory diseases, diabetes, alcoholism, and suicide. Motor vehicle accidents are the largest cause of death before age seventy, followed by heart disease, other types of accidents, and respiratory diseases. The onset of these disorders is related to diet, alcohol, smoking, stress, occupational hazards, and foolish or irrational behavior. These are social, not medical, causes. They are causes that can be reduced only by changes in life-style.

Self-Care: Life-Style of the Future

Today we are aware that a medical policy of "patch 'em up and send 'em home" is not the best way to improve the quality of people's lives and health. A century from now a more holistic approach to health, which is already emerging, will be clearly evident. People will recognize that only through self-care and preventive medicine can they live longer, healthier lives. Daily self-examinations, made easy with the electronic instruments available in the bathrooms of tomorrow, will be a routine for most people from childhood to old age. To reduce the incidence of heart disease, stroke, diabetes, and cancer, the diet of tomorrow will include less meat, fat, salt, and sugar and more fruit, vegetables, fish, and fiber. With relatively few people smoking tobacco or drinking alcohol, lung cancer, respiratory diseases, alcoholism, and depression will become far less common.

In tomorrow's communities psychiatric advice, group therapy, and vocational, personal, family, and genetic counseling, together with the more relaxed atmosphere associated with working at home, will help to reduce the environmental and biological factors that can lead to mental disorders, birth defects, stress, and occupational hazards. Both families and schools will help children develop self-esteem, learn to accept responsibility, and establish a system of self-care.

Increased self-care may mean that people will prescribe their own drugs for such disorders as asthma, ulcers, and arthritis. Computers, available to customers in pharmacies, will allow people to determine for themselves, through a series of computer-generated questions, which drug might best meet their individual needs. At the same time, the computer would check to be sure that interactions among various drugs taken would have no ill effects.

Increased awareness of the importance of physical and mental health will lead people to exercise their minds as well as their bodies. With more leisure time available, personal journals or diaries, letter writing, and novels written for fun as well as for profit will again become popular. Individuals who are knowledgeable in a craft, skill, or topic will contribute their expertise in helping the community. There will be more clubs and organizations devoted to special interests. In addition, more people will have the time and interest required to participate effectively in local government.

Both adults and children will participate in sports and exercise, but there will be less adult supervision of children's sports. Children will be expected to accept more responsibility in organizing their leisure time. Parents will realize that only by doing it themselves can children develop initiative and imagination. Left more to their own, children will invent new games and be more innovative than they are today in a society where children are expected to play organized sports and packaged games developed by adults using rules established by adults.

Early education will take place in a creatively designed place that will allow children to develop their minds and bodies simultaneously. As a result of better early education, family environment, nutrition, health care, and exercise, people throughout society will be more intelligent as well as healthier.

Genetic and chromosomal screening, together with computer analysis of brain waves, will provide early treatment for those born with learning disabilities, autism, or hyperactive tendencies. These techniques may even lead to ways of preventing these problems in the newborn.

The Future of Computers in Medicine

The impact of the computer on medical technology is evident today. The use of computers in medicine will continue to grow. In addition to its present role in keeping records, storing and retrieving information, and guiding and monitoring medical instruments, the computer will help doctors analyze symptoms, diagnose disorders, and prescribe treatments. Its ability to store, relate, and retrieve vast amounts of data makes the computer a far better device for analyzing *all* the facts than is the human brain, with its occasional memory lapses.

The human element, however, will remain an important part of medicine. A computer can assimilate only the information that human minds feed into its memory. As a result, physicians will continue to consult colleagues and use their own ingenious, creative minds in treating patients.

Computer-guided robots will attend to routine hospital chores, leaving nurses and aides free to do more interesting and challenging work. Other robots, unconcerned about the dangers of radiation, will replace surgeons in implanting radioactive pellets into malignant tumors. Computer-guided lasers will aid surgeons in delicate operations and in performing bloodless surgery in which lasers replace scalpels. Computer-controlled insulin pumps implanted beneath the skin of diabetics will monitor blood sugar levels and add insulin at the proper rate. A small computer located behind a patient's ear will monitor heart rate and rhythm, and blood pressure. When appropriate, it will tell the person to reduce his or her activity level, take medication, seek medical help, or, in an emergency, signal paramedics.

Future Medical Technology

Over the next two decades there will probably be dramatic improvements in organ transplants. Yet heart, liver, lung, and pancreas transplant surgery depends on organs being available from recently deceased donors. A century from now, it may be possible to preserve organs by freezing. Banks of hearts, livers, lungs, and kidneys will be available for people in need of transplants. It may also become possible to grow new organs from a single healthy cell obtained from the patient. In that way there will be no problem of tissue rejection. Consequently, there will be little need for the drugs currently used to reduce the body's natural tendency to reject foreign cells.

Depending on the rate of progress in growing replacement organs from the patient's own cells, we may see astounding developments in the design and engineering of artificial organs. Though carefully made, artificial hearts today are plagued by a hard surface, which causes platelets in the patient's blood to break. Since broken platelets release substances that cause blood to thicken, blood clots form and impair circulation in patients with artificial hearts. Medical researchers are looking for a material that will attract the patient's own albumin to form a coating on the inner surface of the artificial organ. Once the heart is coated, the danger of clotting caused by platelet breakage will be dramatically reduced. It is probable that such artificial hearts will precede the growth of replacement organs from the patient's own cells—a development that may be a century away.

A chemical substance found in natural bone, when combined with polyethylene, will provide artificial bone matter compatible with natural bone. It will be used to replace damaged bone or repair bone defects while promoting the growth of surrounding tissue.

Health and Medicine

The complexity of lungs and livers makes it highly unlikely that we will see artificial forms of these organs within the next few decades. However, bionic arms and legs, along with artificial ears, fallopian tubes, penises, corneas, arteries, and skin may become as common as the plastic hip during the next few years. To give recipients control of their artificial limbs, medical engineers hope to electrically amplify the weak nerve impulses that arrive at the limb's stump.

Many believe that it will be possible to amplify the so-called E waves (expectancy waves) of the brain, which are generated before a voluntary action. Paralyzed people could then use these waves to operate switches. Just by thinking about turning on a television set, radio, computer, or some other device, the person could activate electronic switches, thus gaining greater control and independence.

Electronics and chemistry will allow many handicapped people to live a more productive and active life. Memory pills will help everyone, but future brain research will be of greater importance. Scientists will develop chemicals to suppress pain, control rage, and prevent epilepsy, depression, phobias, schizophrenia, and neuroses. Training in biofeedback techniques will allow people to control stress, heart rate, and blood pressure as well as to gain relief from migraine headaches, insomnia, indigestion, epilepsy, and facial tics.

Fine wires leading from a lightweight television camera mounted on a blind person's chest to the rear of the brain will allow that person to see. Wires carrying amplified impulses from the front of the brain to muscles in the limbs will allow a newly paralyzed person to move voluntarily.

As we learn more about the chemistry of life, it may become possible to extend the average life span by at least several decades. It may even be possible to stop the aging process entirely. Some people believe aging is caused by free radicals (chemicals) produced in body cells during the reactions that normally occur there. These free radicals are believed to damage chromosomes, cell membranes, and various proteins. Since a group of chemicals called antioxidants are known to reduce the concentration of free radicals, it is possible that antioxidants could be used to reduce or eliminate aging.

Future Problems in Health Care

Alvin Toffler, in his book, *Future Shock,* warns us about the effects of the rapid rate of change evident in society and technology today and for the foreseeable future. Such change can lead to sensory overload, feelings of insecurity, and instability. Stable and closely knit communities, together with a communication system that will allow people to work at home, will offer some constancy in a future filled with change. If these sources of social and mental stability do not appear, a less pleasant future scenario is likely.

As life expectancy increases through advances in health care and medical technology, the average age of a citizen in this country will rise. The higher cost of medical treatment and the greater number of elderly patients who need such treatment may lead to some form of medical rationing. Should medical care for the aged be limited in order to enhance the care of younger patients? Should high-cost medical service have a cut-off point based on age? Should someone be denied a heart transplant after age sixty? These are ethical questions future generations may have to face.

It is difficult to predict whether medical insurance and/or medical care in this country will be operated by government or free enterprise a century from now. But it is likely that the high cost of equipment and space will lead more doctors to work in groups. Possibly, health maintenance organization (HMO) programs, where people pay a yearly fee for all health care, will flourish. Perhaps independent groups established by the doctors themselves will become increasingly common. What does seem evident is that future health care will be more holistic and will involve considerably more self-care, and that hospital care will be reserved for the very ill. Hospitals will recognize the need for a cheerful setting as well as sophisticated equipment, and they will be pleasanter places than they are today.

Conclusions

As you have read, dramatic changes have taken place during the past century. A hundred years ago most people lived in a rural environment and traveled only short distances by horse and buggy. Today, we can travel half way around the world in a day by airplane, or orbit the earth every 90 minutes in a spaceship. Satellites that remain in fixed positions above the earth enable us to see and hear events such as the Olympic Games even when they are held in distant lands. To see such things as they take place on fields half-a-globe away was beyond the wildest dreams of our nineteenth-century ancestors.

Based on current historical trends and the vast potential of electronic developments, we have "painted" scenarios of the smaller world that your children and grandchildren will find at the close of the twenty-first century. Of course, there will be changes, discoveries, and breakthroughs that we cannot predict. These unknowns will affect the future in unpredictable ways just as computers, lasers, organ transplants, artificial joints, and various other inventions have produced portions of a present never predicted by our ancestors.

We hope you will remember this book and tell your children and grandchildren about it. They may be amazed at some of our predictions. And they will certainly be amused at other predictions of ours that, through the course of history and unforeseen events, will never occur. Perhaps, a century hence, one of your grandchildren will

Conclusions

write a book about what life will be like in 2190 and compare his or her present with the primitive ways of society at the end of the twentieth century. We are assuming, of course, that books will still be a form of communication in 2090.

Books about the Future

*Ardley, Neil. *Our Future Needs.* New York: Franklin Watts, 1982.

Burke, James. *Connections.* Boston: Little, Brown, 1978.

Caddy, Douglas. *Exploring America's Future.* College Station: Texas A & M University Press, 1987.

Calder, Nigel. *Spaceships of the Mind.* New York: Viking, 1978.

Clarke, Arthur C. *July 20, 2019: Life in the 21st Century.* New York: Macmillan, 1986.

*Corn, Joseph J., and Brian Harrigan. *Yesterday's Tomorrows.* New York: Summit Books, 1984.

Fjermedal, Grant. *The Tomorrow Makers.* New York: Macmillan, 1986.

Haas, John D., et al. *Teaching about the Future: Tools, Topics and Issues.* Denver: Social Science Education Consortium and Center for International Relations, 1987.

Morgan, Chris. *Future Man?* New York: Irvington, 1980.

Noble, Halcomb B., ed. *Next: The Coming Era in Science.* Boston: Little, Brown, 1988.

*Taylor, Paula. *The Kids' Whole Future Catalog.* New York: Random House, 1982.

* Readers of The Future and the Past will find these books particularly readable.

Books about the Future

Toffler, Alvin. *Future Shock.* New York: Random House, 1970.

——— *The Third Wave.* New York: Morrow, 1980.

*Wehmeyer, Lillian Biermann. *Futuristics.* New York: Franklin Watts, 1986.

The Futurist, a magazine published bimonthly by the World Future Society, 4916 St. Elmo Avenue, Bethesda, MD 20814, is a journal of forecasts, trends, and ideas about the future.

Books and Articles about the Past

*Bettmann, Otto L. *The Good Old Days: They Were Terrible.* New York: Random House, 1974.

Burnett, John. "The History of Childhood." *History Today,* December 1983.

Burris-Mayer, Elizabeth. *This Is Fashion.* New York: Harper, 1943.

*Cable, Mary. "Bringing Up Baby." *American Heritage,* December 1972.

——— *The Little Darlings: A History of Child Rearing in America.* New York: Scribner's, 1975.

*DeNevi, Don, Charles Smallwood, and Warren Edward Miller. *The Cable Car Book.* New York: Bonanza Books, 1980.

Furnas, J. C. *The Americans: A Social History of the United States 1587–1914.* New York: Putnam, 1969.

Green, Harvey. *The Light of the Home.* New York: Pantheon Books, 1983.

Grow, Lawrence, and Dina VonZweck. *American Victorian.* New York: Harper & Row, 1985.

Heininger, Mary Lynn Stevens. "Children, Childhood and Change in America, 1820–1900." In Mary Lynn Stevens Heininger (ed.), *A Century of Childhood.* Rochester, N.Y.: Margaret Woodbury Strong Museum, 1984.

* *Readers of* The Future and the Past *will find these books particularly readable.*

Lester, Kathleen Morris. *Historic Costume.* Peoria, Ill.: Manual Arts Press, 1925.

*Lewis, Billy C. "The Bells Still Toll for San Francisco's Hills." *American History Illustrated,* April 1987.

Lynes, Russell. "The Parlor." *American Heritage,* October 1963.

Maas, John. *The Victorian House in America.* New York: Hawthorn Books, 1972.

Middleton, William D. "A Century of Cable Cars." *American Heritage,* April–May 1985.

*Moedinger, William M. *The Trolley: Triumph of Transportation.* Lebanon, Pa.: Applied Arts Publishers, 1987.

Rosenberg, Charles E. "What Was It Like to Be Sick in 1884?" *American Heritage,* October–November, 1984.

Rosenzweig, Linda, and Peter Stearns. *Themes in Modern Social History.* Pittsburgh: Carnegie Mellon University Press, 1985.

Schneider, A. Lenore. *The History of Childhood.* Pittsburgh: Carnegie Mellon University Press, 1980.

Seale, William. *The Tasteful Interlude: American Interiors through the Camera's Eye.* Nashville, Tenn.: AASLH, 1984.

*Tarn, Joel A. "Urban Pollution, Many Long Years Ago." *American Heritage,* October 1971.

*Walker, Robert H. *The Age of Enterprise.* New York: Putnam, 1971.

Wilcox, R. Turner. *Five Centuries of American Costume.* New York: Scribner's, 1963.

Wilkie, Jacqueline S. *The History of Health and Medicine.* Pittsburgh: Carnegie-Mellon University Press, 1980.

Index

Adolescence, 39
Air brake, 109
Airplanes, 125–126
Airships, 127
Alger, Horatio, 36
American Federation of Labor (AFL), 71, 72–73
Architecture
  Colonial Revival, 48
  of 1890, 48–50
  front door, 48–49
  of interiors, 49–50
  Queen Anne, 48
  Shingle Style, 48
Assembly line, 70, 119
Automobiles, 118–122

Balloon frame, 47–48
Banking, 29, 59, 80–81
Barry, Leona, 72
Baseball, 19–20
Bathroom, 56–58
Bathtub, 57
Bedroom, 55–56
Bell, Alexander Graham, 99, 100
Bellamy, Edward, 6
Bicycling, 21
Birthrate, 13
Blouses, 94
Books, 35–36
Booth, Edwin, 23

Boxing, 20–21
Breakfast, 133–134
Brooklyn (N.Y.), 116
Bustle, 91

Cable cars, 113–115
Central Park (N.Y.), 40
Cereal, 135
Chairs, 51
Children
  books and magazines, 35–36
  changes in attitude toward, 31–34
  in 1800s U.S., 31–32
  in family, 16–17, 25
  fashions, 94–96
  health care, 34
  juvenile delinquency, 40–41
  labor, 32–33, 74–78
  play, 35
  post-primary school, 43–45
  in 2090, 42–45
Circuses, 23
Clothing. *See* Fashion; specific articles
Collars, 88
Communication, 98–107
  comptelvideo, 102
  and crime, 104–107
  as key to future, 100–102
  satcomptelvideo, 103

Index

Community, 26–27
Computers
  banking, 29, 59, 80–81
  bulletin boards, 27
  comptelvideo, 102
  in court cases, 106
  and crime, 105
  education, 42–44
  in homes, 24, 28, 58–60
  Information Age, 79–80
  and medicine, 153, 154–155
  satcomptelvideo, 103
  and satellites, 103–104
Corsets, 91 92, 94
County fair, 17, 19
Courts, 106
Crime
  communication technology and, 104–109
  data bank on felons, 105
  house arrest, 106
  juvenile delinquency, 40–41
  rehabilitation of criminals, 106–107
  voice prints, 105
Croquet, 21

Delphi technique, 6
De Poele, Charles, 115
Digital signals, 101
Dining room, 53–54
Dresses, 91, 94
Drug abuse, 107, 149–150

Economics, 29
Education
  compulsory, 32, 38
  computers, 42–44
  kindergarten, 33
  as lifelong process, 42
  19th century, 17, 29, 36–38
  parochial, 37–38
  in 2090, 42–45

Electricity, 120
Electromagnets, 122–123
Entertainment, 27–28
Environment, 81–82
Exercise, 28

Factories, 69–70, 75–77
Family, 11
  children, 16–17, 25
  economics, 29
  of 1890, 12–19
  entertainment, 27–28
  extended, 12–13, 46
  father, 14
  mother, 14–16
  nuclear, 12, 25
  of 2090, 24–27
Farming, 129–133, 137–141
Fashion
  children's, 94–95
  men's, 85–89
  of tomorrow, 96–97
  women's, 89–94
Field, Cyrus, 99
Fish farms, 144
Food, 133–137
Football, 20
Ford, Henry, 70, 119
Fruit, 134, 145
Furniture, 51, 55
Future prediction, 4–10

Gangs, 40
Golf, 21
Gompers, Samuel, 71
Greenhouses, 141, 143

Hall, G. Stanley, 39
Hallidie, Andrew S., 113
Hats, 88–89
Health care
  for children, 34

Health care—*Cont.*
  and computers, 153, 154–155
  future problems, 158–159
  19th century, 146–151
  patent medicine, 148–149
  technology, 155–158
  today's, 151
  tomorrow's, 152–159
  transplants, 156
Helium, 119–120
Hine, Lewis, 33, 78
Horse and buggy, 111
Horses, 111–113
Housing
  alternate types of, 60–66
  bathrooms, 56–58
  bedrooms, 55–56
  computers, 58–60
  dining room, 53–54
  in 1890, 47–57
  floating towns, 61–62
  kitchen, 54–55
  parlor, 50–53
  in space, 62–66
  temperature, 53, 59, 60
  underground, 60–61
  undersea, 61
Hydrogen fusion, 119–120, 122

Immigrants, 13
Industrial accidents, 69
Information Age, 79–80
Israel, 138–140

Jobs. *See* Work
Juvenile delinquency, 40–41

Kellogg, John H., 135
Kitchen, 54–55
Knickers, 96

Lasers, 27–28, 105
Lawyers, 106
Leisure, 19–23
Life expectancy, 80
Looking Backward, 6
Lunar products, 83

Magazines, 35–36
Mail-order catalogs, 19
Manure, 112
Marconi, Guglielmo, 99
Mass production, 70
Mass transit, 112–119
  cable cars, 113–115
  elevated trains, 113
  of tomorrow, 124–125
  trolleys, 115–119
McGuffey readers, 37
Melodrama, 23
Middle class, 13
Moneyless society, 80–81
Morse, Samuel F.B., 99
Mother Jones, 72

Natural resources, 81–82
New York City
  crime in, 40
  elevated train, 113
  horsecar, 112
  trolley, 116
Nuclear fusion, 119–120, 122

O'Sullivan, Mary, 73
Overalls, 89

Parlor, 50–53
Photovoltaic cells, 120
Police, 74–75
Postal service, 19
Pullman, George, 109

Radio, 99

Index

Railroads
  as boon to business, 110–111
  dining cars, 110
  elevated trains, 113
  in 19th century, 109–111
  sleeping car, 109
  of tomorrow, 122–123
  transcontinental, 109
Recycling, 82
Riis, Jacob, 33
Rogers, John, 52

San Francisco (Calif.), 113–115
Satellites, 103–104
Scenarios, 7
Science fiction, 6
Scientific management, 70
Shirts, 86, 88, 89
Shoes, 92–93
Social historians, 2–3
Space, 28, 62–66
Spock, Benjamin, 41
Sports, 19–22, 28
Sprague, Frank J., 116
Stereoscope, 35
Stove, 54
Strikes, 72
Suits, 85–86
Sullivan, John L., 21
Superconductors, 122

Taylor, Frederick W., 70
Teenagers, 38–40, 45
Telegraph, 98–99
Telephone, 98–101
Television, 27–28
Tennis, 21
Textbooks, 36–37

Theater, 22–23
Toys, 35
Transportation. *See* Mass transit; specific means of transportation
Trolleys, 115–119
Trucks, 122

Underwear, 85

Vaccination, 150
Vaudeville, 23
Videotelephones, 101–102

Wallpaper, 51
Washstand, 55
Waste materials, 82
Water, 137–140, 141
Watkins, John E., 8–10
Westinghouse, George, 109
Women
  of 1890s, 15–16, 91, 93
  farm, 131
  fashions, 89–94
  sports, 22, 93
  work, 72–74
Work
  absenteeism, 71
  accidents, 69
  change in nature of, 68–72, 78–79
  child labor, 32–33, 74–78
  early view of, 67–68
  on farm, 68
  at home, 24–25, 28
  in Information Age, 79–80
  picketing, 71
  strikes, 72
  unions, 71
  wages, 69
  women and, 72–74

About the Authors

ROBERT GARDNER is head of the science department at Salisbury School, Salisbury, Connecticut, where he teaches physics, chemistry, and physical science. He did his undergraduate work at Wesleyan University and has graduate degrees from Trinity College and Wesleyan University. He has taught in a number of National Science Foundation teachers' institutes and is the author of several science books, including *Kitchen Chemistry; Projects in Space Science; Water, The Life Sustaining Resource;* and *The Whale Watchers' Guide.*

DENNIS SHORTELLE is a history teacher at Salisbury School, Salisbury, Connecticut. He did his undergraduate work at St Anselm's College and has graduate degrees from Niagara and Wesleyan Universities.